at a Time

A Beginner's Guide

Tricia Sutton

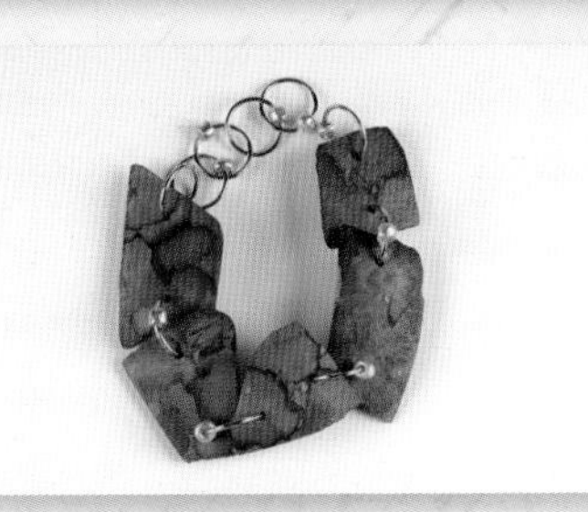

4880 Lower Valley Road • Atglen, PA 19310

Library of Congress Control Number: 2012940984

Designed by **Danielle D. Farmer**
Cover Design by **RoS**
Type set in Britannic Bold/Avenir LT Std

ISBN: 978-0-7643-4146-5
Printed in China

Published by Schiffer Publishing, Ltd.
4880 Lower Valley Road
Atglen, PA 19310
Phone: (610) 593-1777; Fax: (610) 593-2002
E-mail: Info@schifferbooks.com

For the largest selection of fine reference books on this and related subjects, please visit our website at: ***www.schifferbooks.com.***
You may also write for a free catalog.

This book may be purchased from the publisher.
Please try your bookstore first.

We are always looking for people to write books on new and related subjects.
If you have an idea for a book, please contact us at
proposals@schifferbooks.com

Schiffer Books are available at special discounts for bulk purchases for sales promotions or premiums. Special editions, including personalized covers, corporate imprints, and excerpts can be created in large quantities for special needs. For more information contact the publisher.

In Europe, Schiffer books are distributed by
Bushwood Books
6 Marksbury Ave.
Kew Gardens
Surrey TW9 4JF England
Phone: 44 (0) 20 8392 8585; Fax: 44 (0) 20 8392 9876
E-mail: info@bushwoodbooks.co.uk
Website: www.bushwoodbooks.co.uk

Acknowledgments

I thank Kendel, Joseph III, BrookLynn, and Stephen for their encouragement, love, and support, and I thank Paula, Bob, Joseph III, and Jessica for proofreading.

I thank Ann Reilly for her suggestions of some of the projects and content featured here. Without her help, this book might never have been started.

Other Schiffer Books on Related Subjects:

Apples to Apples: Basic Techniques for Decorating Gourds,
978-0-7643-3621-8, $19.99

Gourd Art Basics: The Complete Guide to Cleaning, Preparation, and Repair,
978-0-7643-2829-9, $14.99

Gourd Crafts: 6 Projects & Patterns,
978-0-7643-2825-1, $14.95

Gourd Fun for Everyone,
978-0-7643-3124-4, $22.99

Contents

Introduction

A few years ago, a friend and I were new to gourd art. We looked for gourd books to buy, checked libraries, roamed through used book stores, and searched the internet. After buying several books, we discovered that gourd book authors assumed readers had some knowledge of gourds, which we did not. We also discovered authors used electrical equipment neither of us owned.

This book was created in an attempt to help those new to gourd art. Readers will find projects designed to use basic materials and supplies already found in their homes or that can be inexpensively purchased. Follow along step-by-step and enjoy the world of gourd art.

Resources and materials are from:

- **Bayou Gourds** (www.bayougourds.com): clean gourds of all sizes
- **The Caning Shop** (www.caning.com): gourd supplies and equipment, basket supplies, dried naturals, books, wood burning equipment, and wax resist supplies
- **Gluesmith Co.** (www.thegluesmith.com): super glue and accelerator
- **Hobby Lobby** (www.hobbylobby.com) and **Jo-Ann Fabrics** (www.joannfabrics.com): craft supplies
- **Michaels** (www.michaels.com): feathers, craft supplies

Preparing the Gourd

CHAPTER 1

Before starting on the projects featured in this book, consider the following suggestions for preparing the gourd to be cut, punctured, or, very simply, decorated. Working outside or in a well-ventilated area will be helpful because there can be a lot of dust when cleaning and cutting. It's also a good idea to use dust masks, goggles, and disposable gloves for protecting your nose, mouth, eyes, and hands.

Once a "tool," such as a kitchen knife, has been used on a gourd, it should no longer be used on food. Keep gourd tools, utensils, and containers separate from other household items.

When purchasing gourds, search for the cleanest ones to keep your cleaning time to a minimum. The shapes of gourds and the names associated with those shapes can vary. The American Gourd Society website (www.americangourdsociety.org) contains helpful information relating to shapes, as well as sources for purchasing gourds. In this book, familiar names for shapes will be used.

Cleaning the Gourd's Exterior

Materials Needed:

- sand paper, various grits
- pot scrubbers: copper, brass, aluminum
- disposable or household plastic gloves
- steel wool
- old toothbrushes, dish brush
- table knife (tape over serrated edge)
- wire brush
- blunt letter opener
- dust mask
- plastic goggles
- detergent
- water
- cleansing powder
- potting soil without additives

Respirator mask, paper masks, goggles, sandpaper, and emery boards

Copper mesh scrubber, wire brush, and toothbrush

▶ TIP:

When using an old table knife to scrape off the skin or dirt from a gourd, tape over the serrated edge with masking tape. The serration can mar the smooth surface of the gourd. Other times you may want the "marks" to enhance your finished piece.

POTTING SOIL CLEANING METHOD

Materials Needed

- plastic bin with lid
- water
- potting soil without additives

In very hot weather, gourds will be ready in two days. Once the weather turns cooler, it may take up to five days. Add water as needed to keep the soil damp. When gourds are removed from the container, rinse off the dirt. Use a pot scrubber or other scraper to remove the skin. Rinse often with clean water as you go. Finish by rubbing the entire surface with a pot scrubber to clean any areas you may have missed. If the skin does not come off easily, return gourds to the container, cover with wet soil, and wait a day or two more.

1. Use a container large enough to accommodate the gourds you are cleaning. Place about two inches of cheap, basic potting soil in the container.

2. Wet soil with water and add a layer of gourds. Layer gourds and soil, making sure that the wet potting soil covers each layer of gourds. The soil needs to be very wet to stick to the gourds. End with a layer of soil to cover gourds being sure to wet this also and then put lid on tightly.

3. Rinse off clinging potting soil. Scrub with scrubber, rinsing frequently to remove gourd skin.

WATER CLEANING TECHNIQUE

Materials needed:

- bucket or plastic tub
- dinner plate
- unopened can goods
- water

While wet, scrape the surface to remove additional blemishes and skin. Once clean, mark your cut line as gourds cut extremely easily when wet. If you are not cutting the gourd or ready to begin decorating, let the gourd dry at least 24 hours.

1. Choose a container large enough to hold gourds being cleaned.

2. Fill the container with water to completely cover gourds.

3. Put heavy items such as canned goods on a plate and set both pieces on top of gourds, making sure the gourds are completely submerged. After several hours, use a scrubber to remove any clinging gourd skin.

CLEANSER CLEANING METHOD

Materials needed:

- cleansing powder
- bucket or container
- small dish
- water
- metal scrubber

This is the quickest of the cleaning methods. When time is a factor, try this method first.

1. Make a thick paste of cleanser and water.

2. Wet gourd thoroughly and scrub surface with a mesh scrubber dipped into the paste. Rinse often and continue scrubbing with paste until surface feels smooth.

Please Read Carefully:

When cutting a gourd, there are several things to consider. Not only will you have dust in the air from the actual cutting process, but you will also find seeds and debris inside the gourd. There can be health issues that occur when working with gourds. The American Gourd Society published information regarding this issue. Before cutting your first gourd, learn about this health information. The AGS can be found online at www.americangourdsociety.org.

After reading the health article, it is time to gather the supplies you will need: goggles or glasses, a mask and gloves. Look at the cutting aids listed below and choose the ones you plan to use.

Once your gourd has been cut, the inside needs to be cleaned. Cleaning the inside of the gourd can be done dry or wet. Either method will work, but sometimes the fact that the gourd is wet on the inside and will keep down the dust is a reason to use a wet soaking method. You can use a variety of items in your home to complete this step. Remember to use goggles or glasses, a mask, and gloves.

Some gourd artists sand the inside of the gourd, especially if it will be used as a bowl or vase. Others paint the inside after scraping, if the inside will be seen.

CUTTING AIDS

Materials needed:

- pencil
- face mask, eye covering, gloves
- masking tape
- flexible ruler
- rubber bands
- embroidery hoop
- books
- bricks
- pieces of wood

As a beginning gourd artist, you may choose to use hand saws for cutting. These can be found at hardware stores and from gourd tool supply companies. Later, if you wish to include power tools for cutting, you will find those at most home improvement stores.

1. Before cutting, a rubber band can be placed on the gourd to mark where the pencil line can be drawn.

2. An embroidery hoop also works well to mark circles on gourds, especially at an angle.

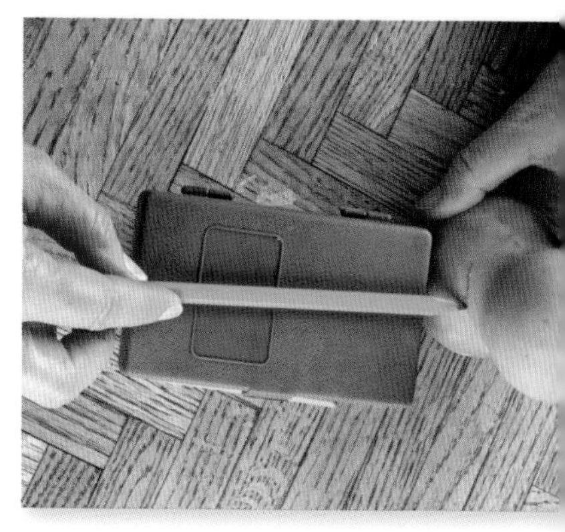

3. To draw a cut line around the gourd a consistent distance from the gourd base, use any flat, even item that attains height needed for pencil line. A stack of books, bricks, or pieces of wood will work for this purpose.

1. Craft knife with assorted blades

CUTTING IMPLEMENTS

Materials needed:

- craft knife
- box cutter
- small hand saws
- wood burning tool and assorted tips
- awl
- mini jig-saw (electric)
- bread knife
- steak knife
- safety gloves

1. Craft knife with assorted blades

2. Box cutter and heavy duty knife

3. Wood burning tool with multiple tips

4. Hand saw and gourd saw

5. Safety gloves with rubberized palms

2. Box cutter and heavy duty knife

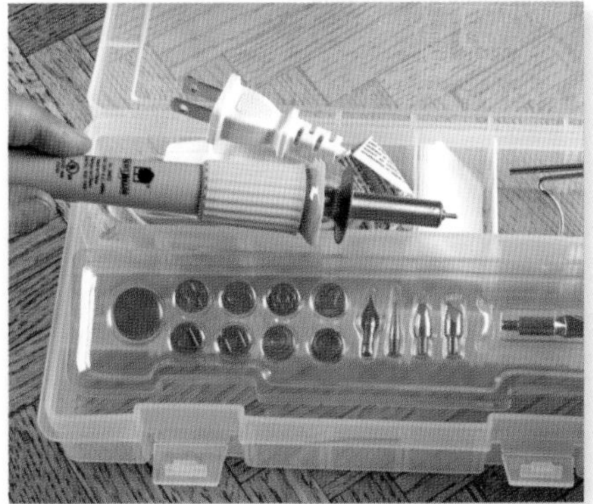
3. Wood burning tool with multiple tips

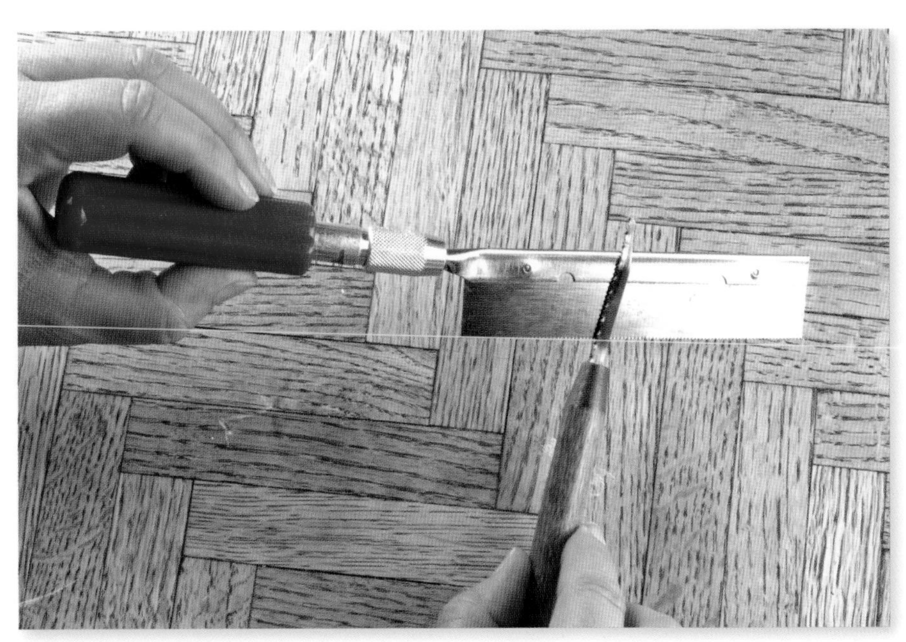
4. Hand saw and gourd saw

5. Safety gloves with rubberized palms

Cleaning the Gourd's Interior

Reminder:
Any kitchen item used in gourd cleaning should never be used again for cutting or preparing food!

Materials needed:

- 1 piece ice cream scoop
- melon scooper
- pumpkin scooper
- 1/4" chisel
- 1/2" chisel
- sturdy forks, knives, spoons
- face and eye protection
- assorted protective hand covering
- commercial gourd scraper

1. Insert craft knife into pencil line and make deep cut long enough to accommodate saw (about one and a half inches).

DRY EASY CUTTING

▶ NOTE:

Smaller gourds might be fragile after they have been cut in half, so work slowly and carefully when making holes and wood burning.

2. Insert saw into cut made by craft knife and slowly cut along pencil line until you meet opening cut.

3. Opened gourd showing fiber and seeds.

4. Fill gourd with liquid detergent and water to rim. This step makes scraping easier.

5. Scrape remaining wet fibers until all are removed. When dry, these fibers are generally white or light in color so you can see when no more remain.

WET EASY CLEANING

When finishing the inside of your gourd, consider one of the following techniques. You may spray paint the inside of the gourd, paint it with a brush, or you may decoupage it with paper or fabric. Any of these techniques will enhance the look of the inside of your gourd.

1. Fiber was removed on right gourd. Fiber remains on left gourd.

2. Halves can be used to create bowls.

Puncturing

Materials needed:

- awls, different sizes
- screwdrivers, assorted sizes
- needle nose pliers
- power drill
- hand drill
- metal or wood skewers

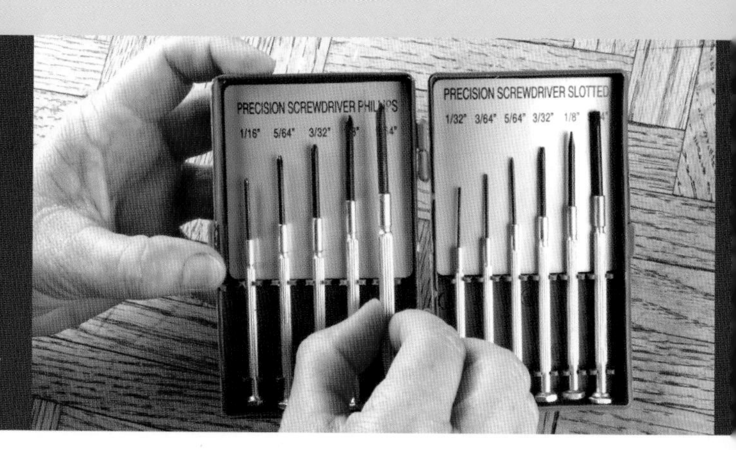

1. Mini screw driver set.

2. Electric drill and awl.

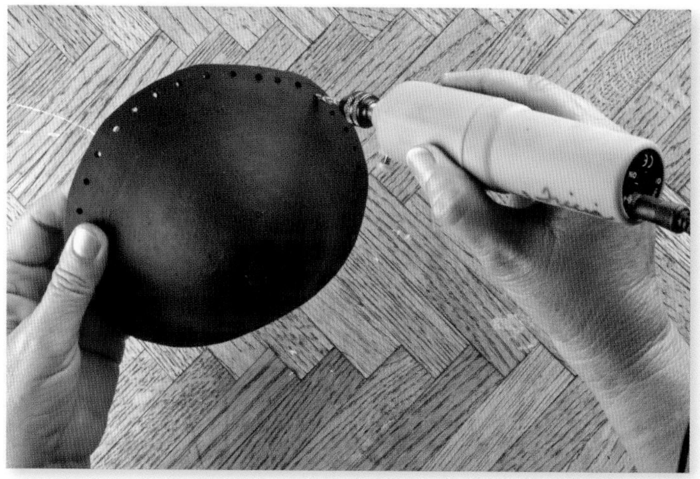

3. Gourd piece with holes made with drill.

4. Drilled holes provide a place for adding beads by using a waxed linen that is "whip stitched" over gourd edge.

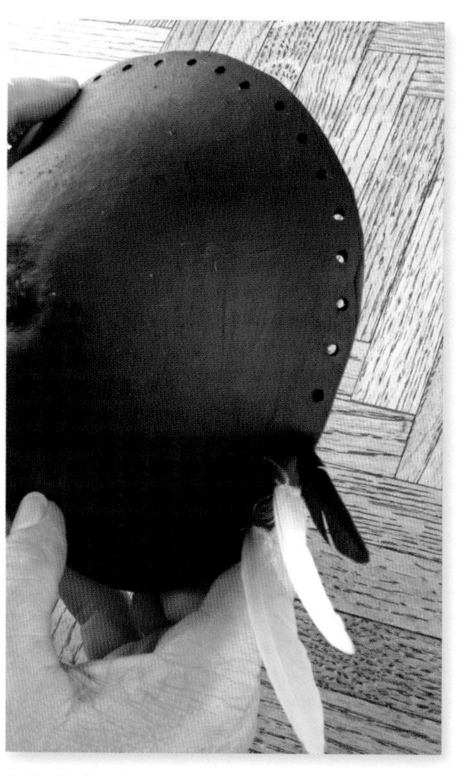

5. Drilled holes also provide a place for feathers to be inserted into a gourd.

Uncleaned Gourd projects

CHAPTER 2

Now you are ready to start decorating a gourd. If you don't want to buy any supplies except the gourd, here are four projects you can do using supplies you may already own. You should be able to complete each of these projects in less than a day.

Snowman Gourd

Materials needed:

- small bottle gourd
- white acrylic paint
- a piece of sponge
- green child's sock, size 12-18 months
- 4-5 mm black pompoms
- 1/2" orange pipe cleaner
- 1" x 8" piece of green felt
- scissors
- glue

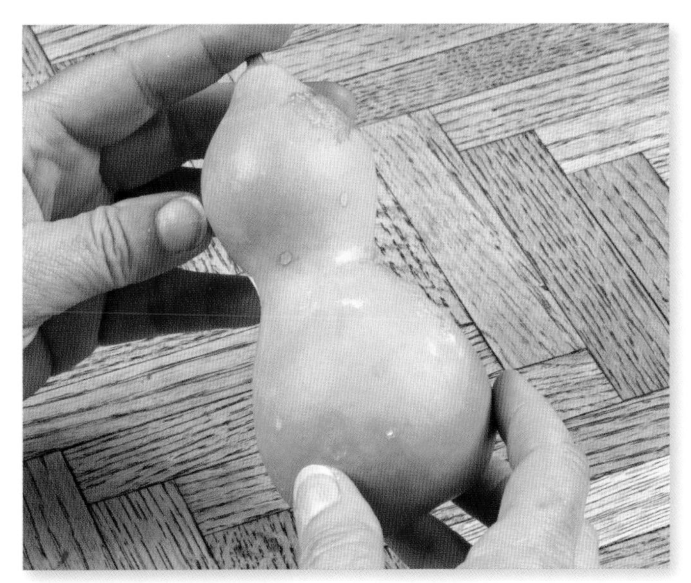

1. Begin with a bottle gourd.

2. Using a small piece of sponge, begin rubbing on white paint.

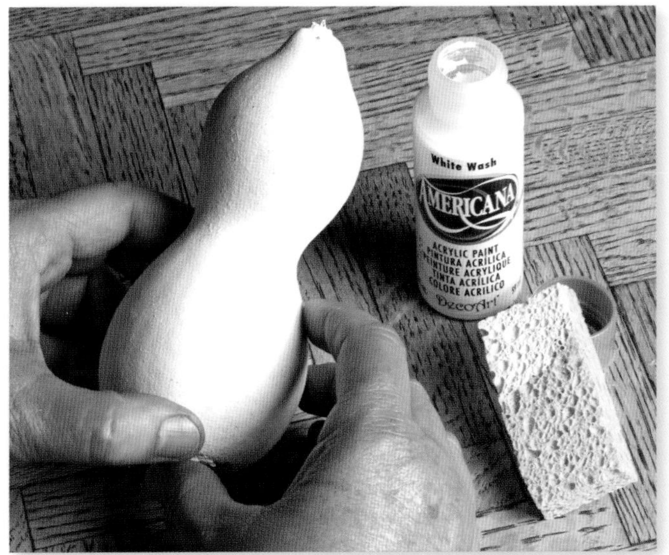

3. After applying two coats of white paint, decide if the coverage pleases you. Using the sponge in a dabbing motion will produce a textured surface. Allow to dry.

4. The toe end of a baby sock (size 12 to 18 months) can be used to form a hat. Cut toe end from sock.

5. Roll up the cut edge of sock and glue on to head end of gourd

6. Glue on pompoms for eyes and buttons.

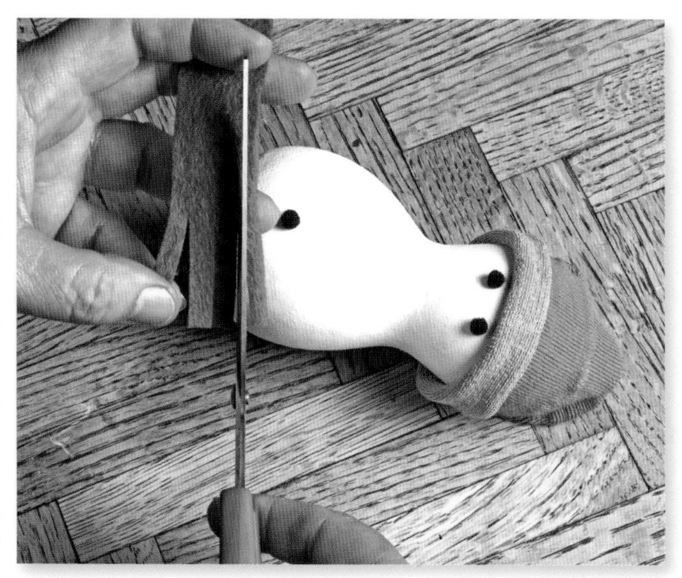

7. Cut felt for scarf. One inch cuts can be made in the ends of felt for fringe.

8. Tie or glue scarf around neck.

9. Glue on orange pipe cleaner for nose.

Paper Decoupage on a Gourd

Materials needed:

- 3″ egg gourd
- any decorative paper, 1 sheet or scraps
- craft glue
- foam brush
- hair dryer
- flat back crystals, any color
- lightweight wire or clear fishing line, 4″ long

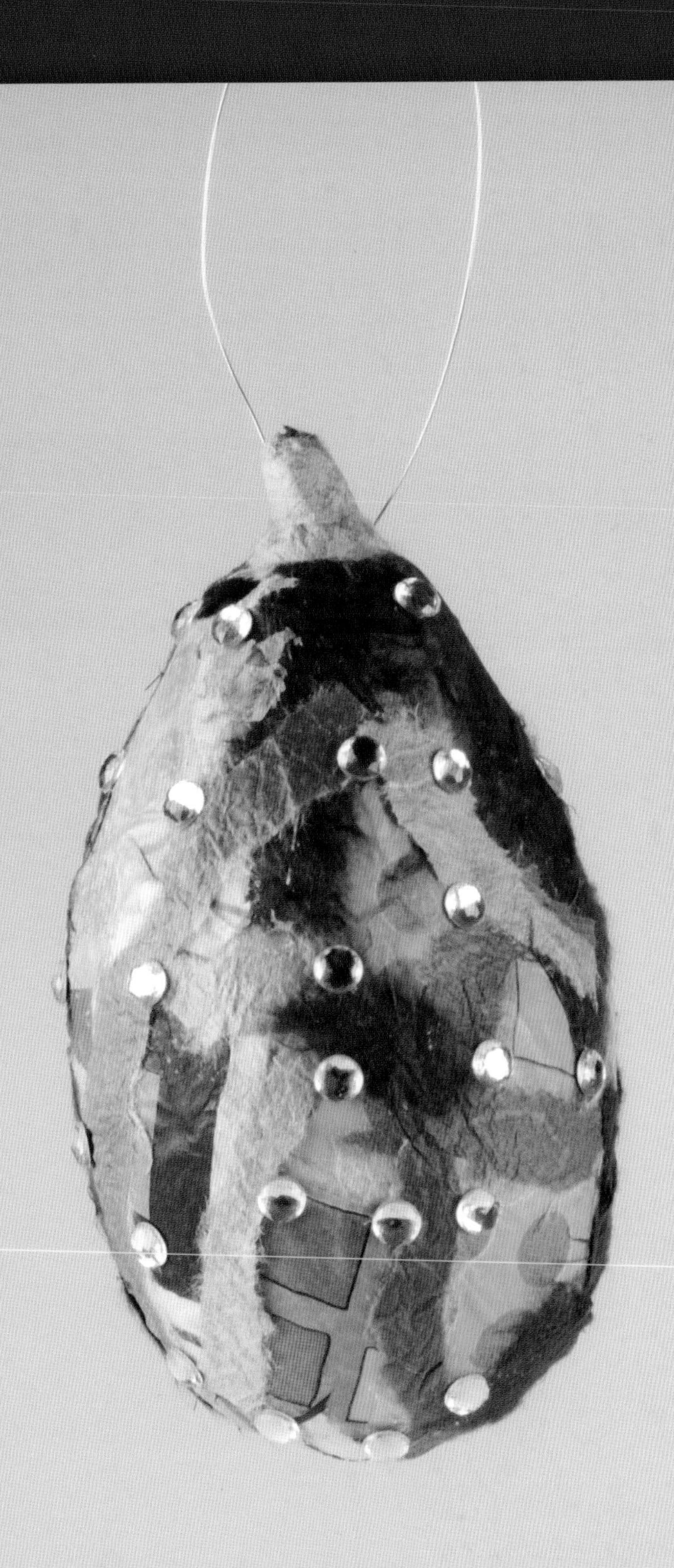

1. Begin with an egg shaped gourd.

2. Apply glue to gourd with a foam brush and add base coat of lightweight or tissue paper.

3. Using one small piece at a time, glue paper to the surface of the gourd.

4. As the pieces are applied, add glue on top of the paper to adhere edges of paper. Slight wrinkles add interesting texture. Glue dries clear.

5. Allow glue to dry thoroughly. A hair dryer can be used to speed up drying time.

6. Randomly glue crystals over paper. A piece of lightweight wire or clear fishing line can be glued to end of gourd for hanging.

▶ TIP:

A hair dryer is a great help in drying paint, sealer, and some dyes and glues.

Feather Covered Gourd

Materials needed:

- egg gourd
- assorted feathers
- craft glue
- 6" leather lacing

1. Begin with egg shaped gourd.

2. Choose the feather colors you plan to use.

3. Starting at the bottom, glue on a row of feathers all around the gourd.

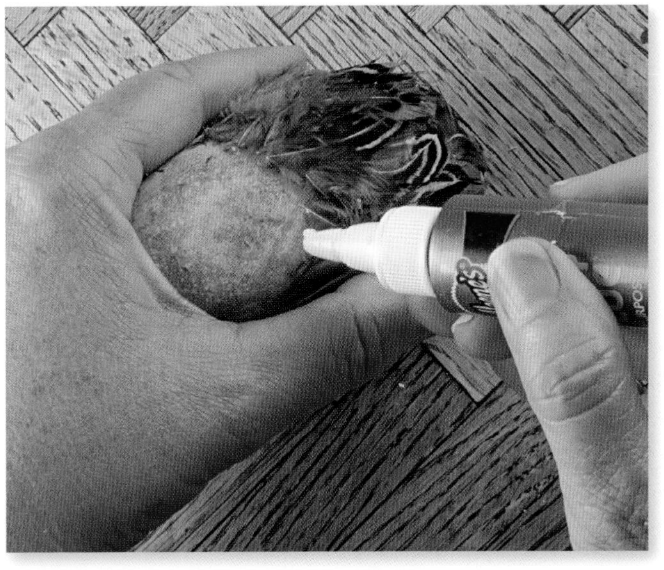

4. Begin second row by overlapping feathers.

5. Continue gluing rows of feathers until entire gourd is covered.

6. Glue both ends of leather strip on top end of gourd.

Clay and Gourd Fish

Materials needed:

- · small banana gourd
- · acrylic paint
- · 2-oz. polymer clay, any color
- · roller (heavy glass or piece of dowel)
- · texturing sheets or fork
- · awl
- · 2 toothpicks
- · toaster oven plus rack or pan
- · 2 flat back crystals
- · plastic glove
- · craft glue
- · 6″ of 20 gauge wire

1. Choose a small banana gourd.

2. Choose a clay color.

3. Condition and roll out clay. Rolling pin, heavy glass, or heavy dowel may be used to roll clay flat.

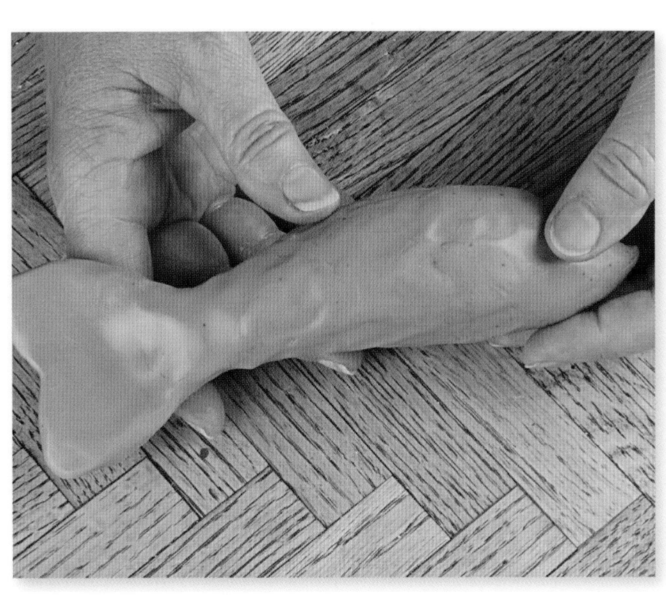

4. Wrap clay around gourd to resemble a fish.

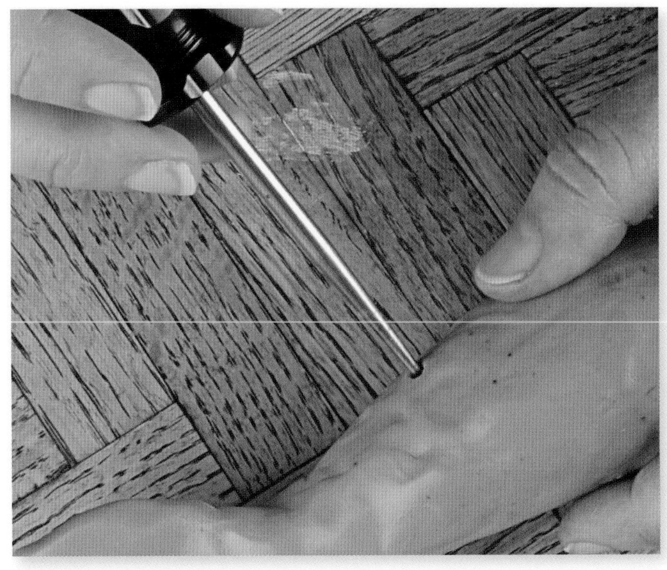

5. Using an awl, make a hole in the gourd near tail.

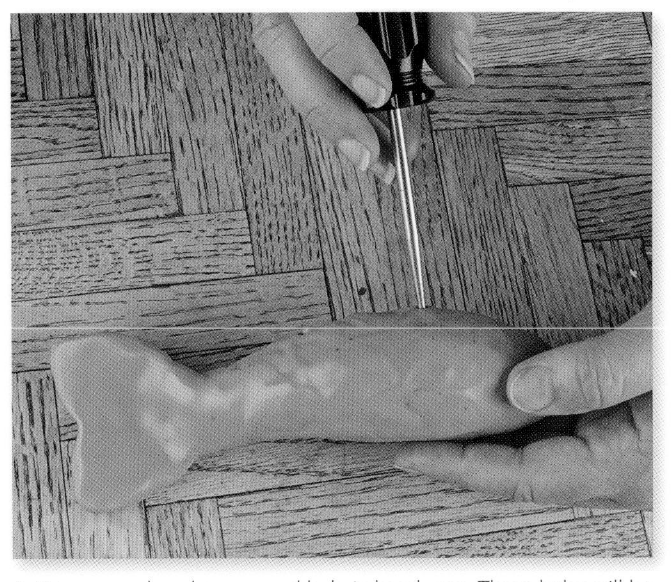

6. Using an awl, make a second hole in head area. These holes will be used later to place hanging wire.

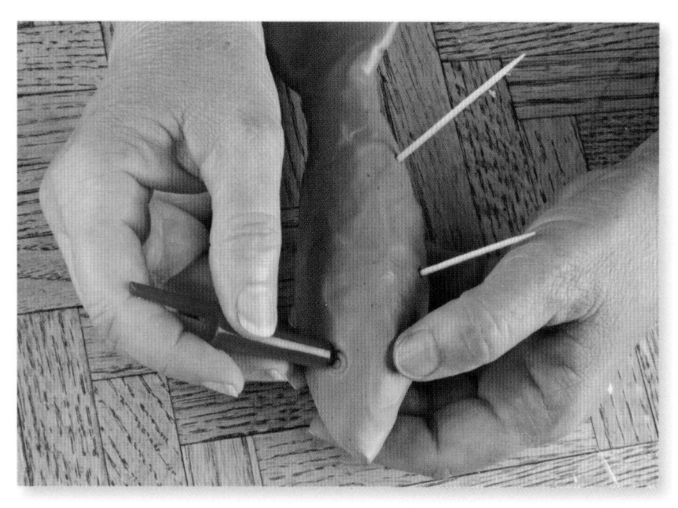

7. Place toothpicks in holes to prevent holes from closing during texturing. Make a depression in clay for eye.

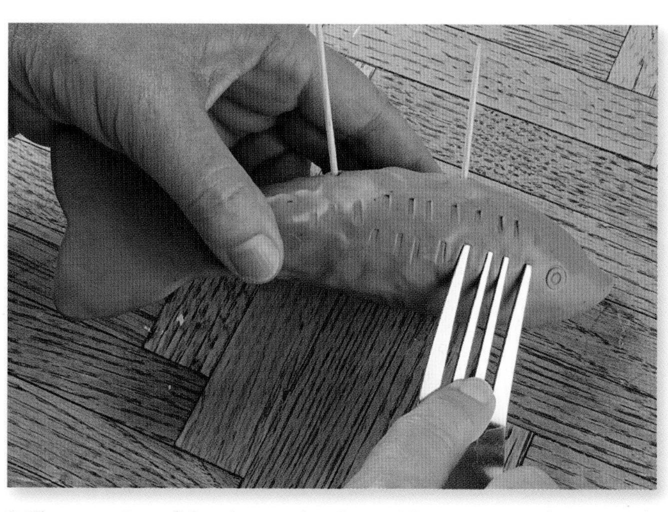

8. The texturing of the clay can be done with a texturing sheet or with items found in the home such as a fork.

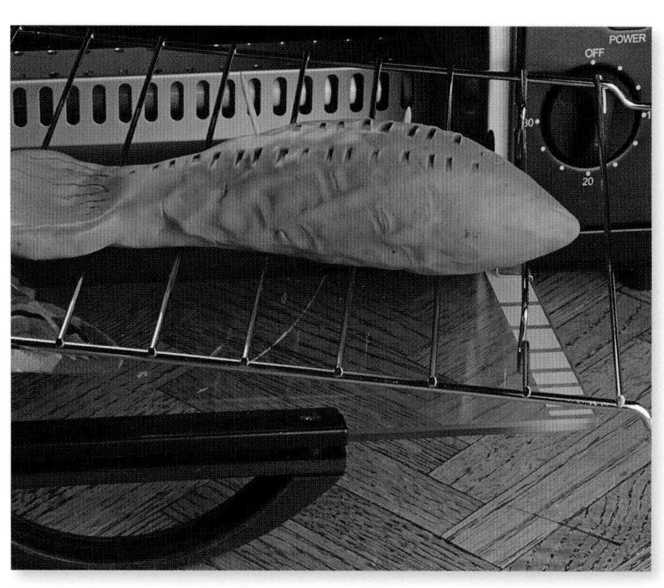

9. Bake clay covered gourd in oven according to manufacturer's directions found on clay packaging. Remove from oven and allow clay to cool.

10. Remove toothpicks. Apply a small amount of paint to one area of clay surface. Using gloved hand, gently rub paint across raised areas created by the texturing process. Continue in this manner until all raised areas of gourd have been painted.

11. Glue eye crystal into depression in clay.

12. Glue hanger in holes made by toothpicks.

More work will be required in this chapter. Each project should reflect your taste and ideas for coloring and enhancement. Feel free to substitute gourd shapes, colors, techniques, and any additional enhancement items.

Gourd Chili

Materials needed:

- cleaned banana gourd
- green acrylic paint
- 2 thumbtacks
- flat back, plastic crystals
- 6" piece of light weight wire
- glue
- brush

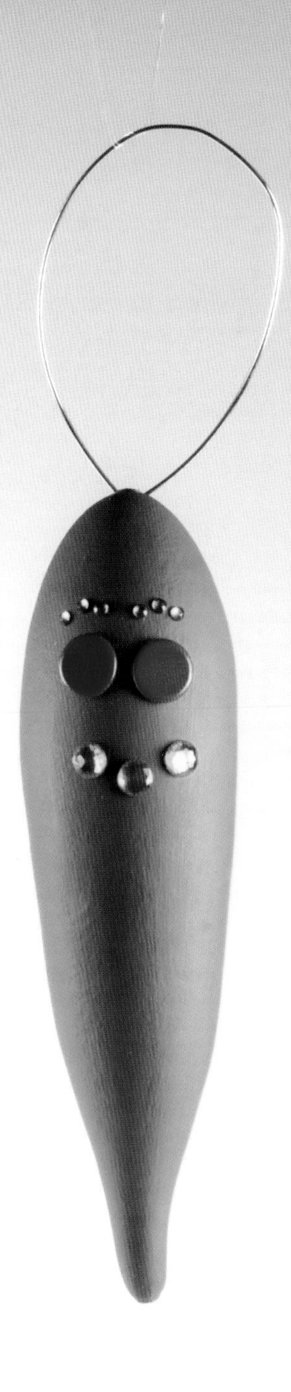

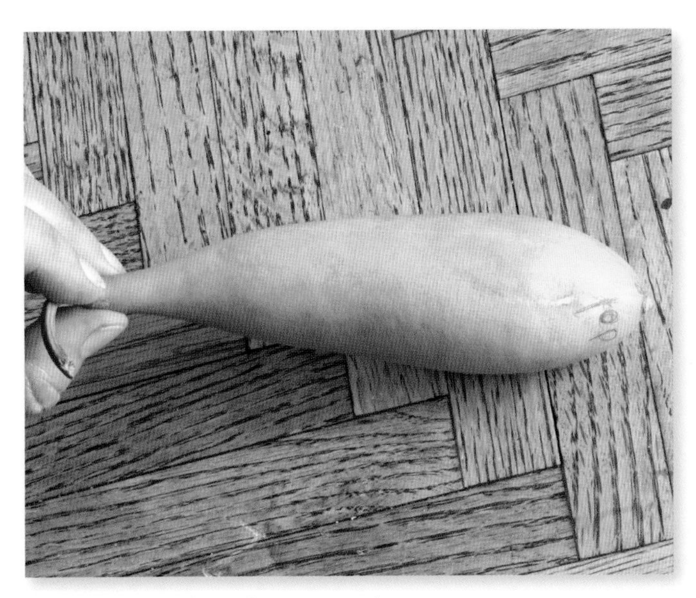

1. This is a cleaned, mini banana gourd.

2. Gourd is covered with your color choice of acrylic paint. More than one coat may be needed. Allow to dry.

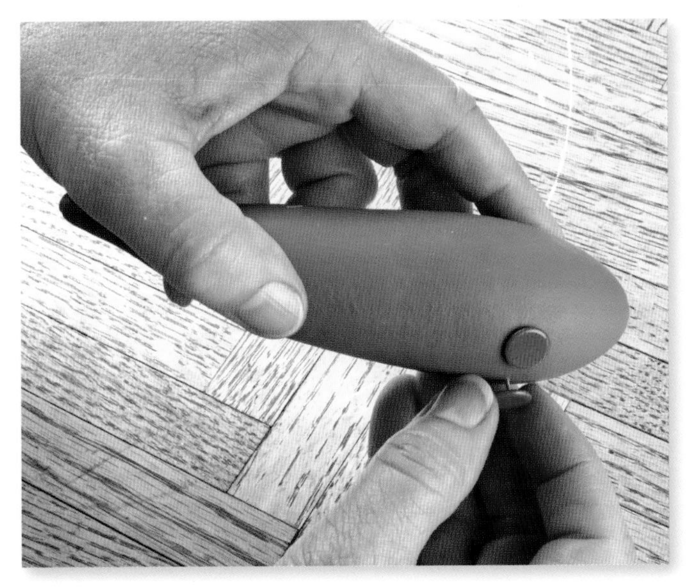

3. Thumb tacks are pressed into gourd for eyes.

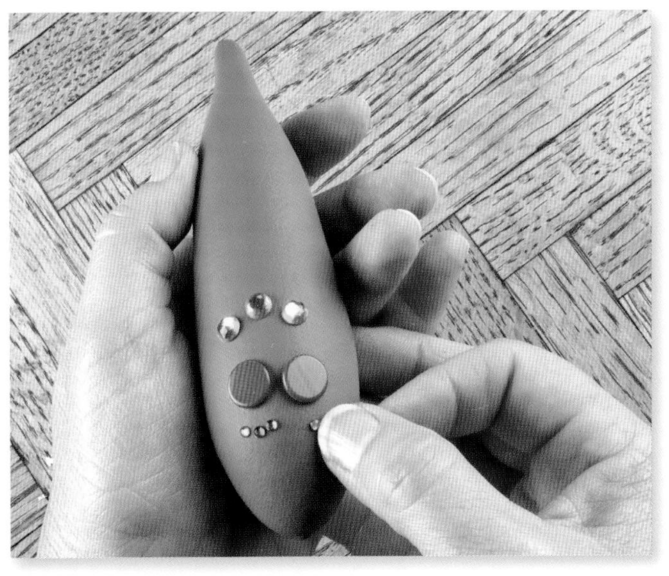

4. Flat backed crystals are glued on for mouth and eyebrows. The number of crystals will be determined by the size crystals used.

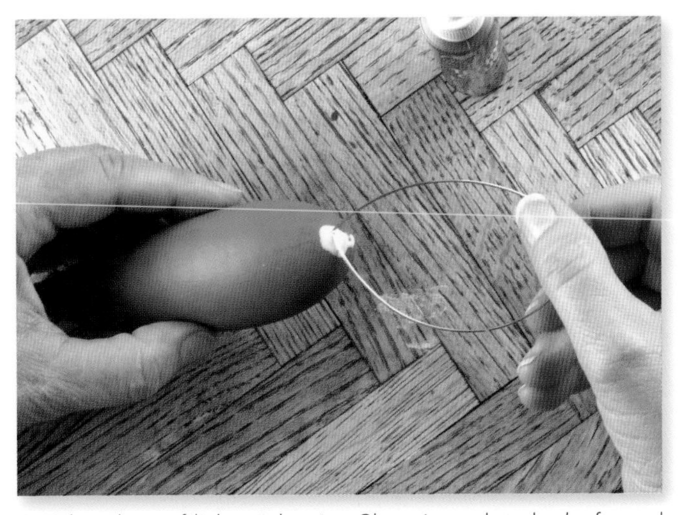

5. Make a loop of lightweight wire. Glue wire ends to back of gourd top. Allow to dry.

Gourd Cat

Materials needed:

- cleaned bushel or pear gourd with stem
- glue
- pencil
- sand paper
- piece of sponge
- black paint pen, green paint pen
- 2-3 colors of acrylic paint for body
- gourd scraps for ears

1. Choose a cleaned bushel or pear gourd with a stem. If needed, a stem from your collection of gourd scraps can be glued in place.

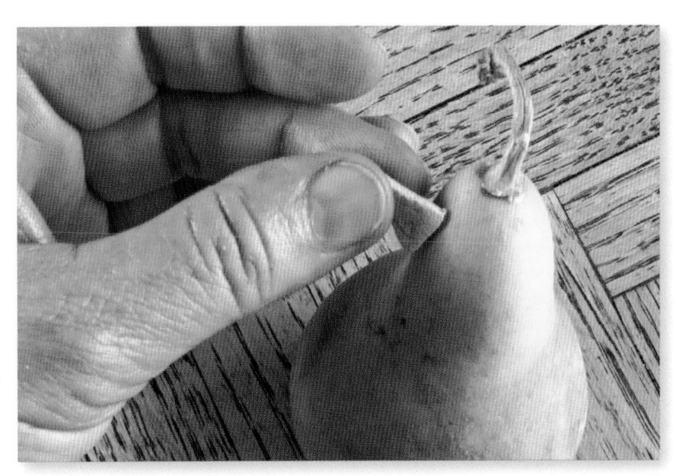

2. Find triangle shaped gourd scraps to make ears. Sand edges and backs of ear pieces. Hold triangle pieces of gourd in place to check for correct size.

3. Refer to picture of finished cat for placement of ears. Sanded sides of gourd pieces face forward and slightly downward. Position ear pieces and mark placement of ears with pencil.

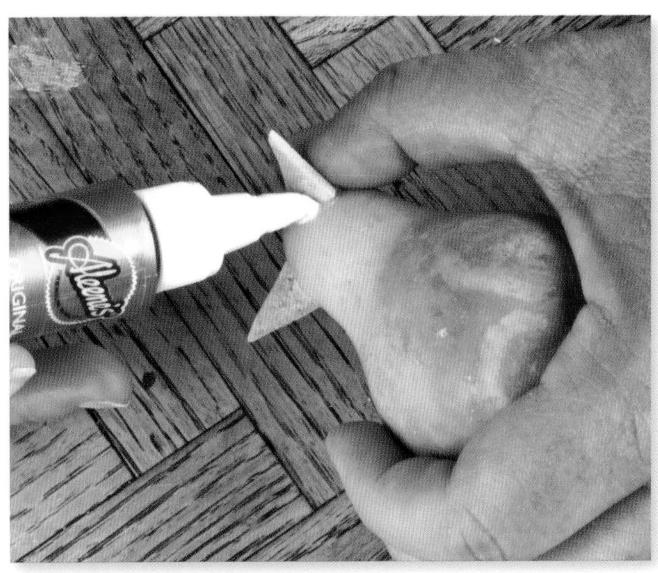

4. Using glue, attach ears to gourd. Wait for glue to dry.

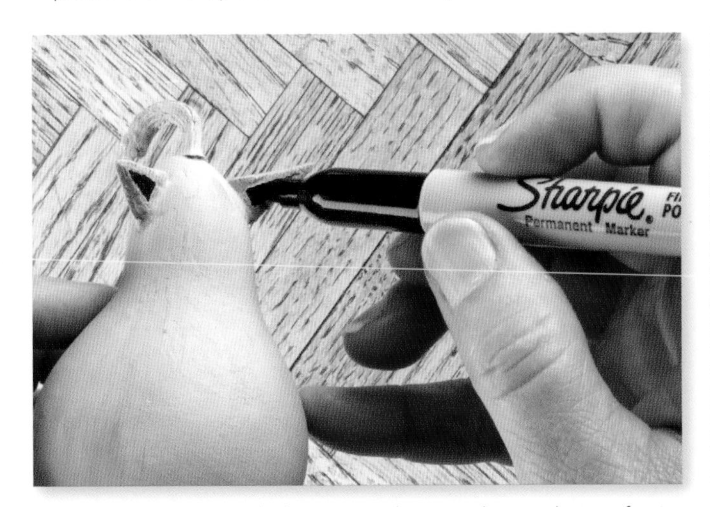

5. Paint entire gourd, including ears and stem with your choice of paint color. Allow to dry. Paint inside of ears black.

6. Use a piece of sponge to dab on two coordinating colors of paint in a random design.

7. Referring to finished cat, sketch eyes, whiskers, nose, and mouth with pencil.

8. Use marker to complete face.

9. Use green marker for green eyes.

Gourd Spirit Figure

Materials needed:

- cleaned bottle gourd
- acrylic paint
- white paint pen
- 8" piece 26 gauge craft wire
- (20) size 6 beads
- sponge piece
- acrylic sealer
- scissors
- wire cutters
- feather
- leather lacing
- 2" x 3" piece of fabric

1. Choose a cleaned mini bottle gourd. Any discoloration in gourd color will be hidden under paint.

2. Paint entire gourd with one or two coats of paint. Allow to dry.

3. Refer to finished picture and, using contrasting color paint pen, draw face and body design using short straight lines, dots, and small curved lines. Starting at the top stem end and working downward makes it easier to paint design. Allow to dry.

4. Spray on light coat of acrylic sealer and allow to dry.

5. Thread beads onto wire and wrap around neck of gourd. Move beads to front of gourd and align with face. At back of gourd neck, twist wire ends tightly to secure beads around neck and glue beads in place. Cut off remaining wire when glue has dried.

6. Glue 2" x 3" piece of fabric around gourd "neck" like a cape, starting at center back and pulling each side forward.

7. Glue feather on top of gourd.

8. Fabric piece is glued at back, around feather. See finished spirit figure for leather lacing tied around feather and stem.

Gourd Bird on Nest

Materials needed:

- cleaned egg gourd with at least a 1/2" stem attached
- acrylic paints, three colors
- 3" grapevine wreath
- small paint brush
- glue
- feather
- black marker
- sponge

1. Choose a small, cleaned egg gourd with an attached 1/2" stem.

2. Paint body of gourd with one to two coats of your choice of paint color. Allow to dry.

3. With wooden end of paint brush, pick up small amount of contrasting paint color and randomly make dots on body of gourd.

4. With sponge, paint beak black.

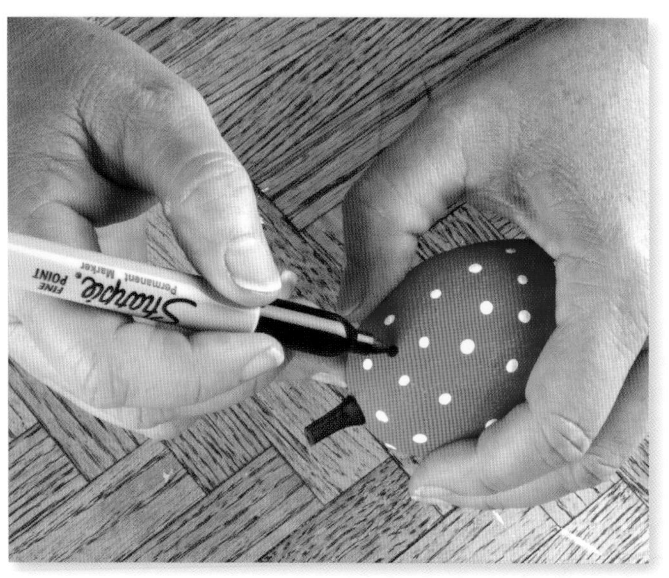

5. With black marker, make small dot for eye on each side of head.

6. Glue feathers near head and tail.

7. Color 3" round grapevine wreath with black paint. Sit or glue bird on "nest."

Coloring & Decorating

CHAPTER 4

In this chapter you are given an overview showing how to color and adorn your gourd projects using a variety of materials and applications. This will give you just a few ideas for creating your own finished gourd projects. Use these suggestions as a starting point and add other techniques and embellishments to these lists.

Resists, paints, dyes, inks, and glazes are some of the products that can be used for coloring your gourds. On the following pages, you will find lists of items and pictures showing some of these items and techniques. As you discover other products you enjoy using, add them to these lists.

Before purchasing anything, search your home for coloring agents, such as teas, coffees, nuts, and vegetable and egg dyes. Experiment with these "colors" to see how you like the results. Keeping a small sample, with a label identifying what was used, can help you make decisions later on when choosing a coloring option.

When you are deciding on color combinations, it can be helpful to wander around the aisles of shops and boutiques. See what colors in clothing and jewelry work well together. If you carry a small card or notebook with you, jot down combinations that are pleasing to you. Later, when you wish to decorate your gourds, you can refer to these color ideas.

Gourd books and websites are valuable sources for decorative techniques. Later in this book you will find some resources utilized for the techniques employed in the projects in Chapters 2, 3, and 5. Gourd classes offer a wealth of ideas for decorating gourds. These are also great places to share ideas. If classes are not offered near your home, you might check the internet for online classes and tutorials. Visiting gourd festivals will also alert you to decorative techniques gourd artists are employing. Then, if you decide to venture into commercial products for your own gourd decorating, you will already have some ideas.

Resists can provide a variety of decorative effects to enhance your gourd project. Their purpose is to mask a part of your design for later removal. When adding your design to a gourd, do not write or draw directly on the gourd surface. These marks cannot be removed once wax has been applied to the gourd.

WAX

Materials needed:

- gourd
- kitska
- tea light candle
- grater or knife
- beeswax or wax melt (darker colors work best)
- matches
- brush-on varnish
- paper towels
- hair dryer

Lit taper candles will create a resist by dripping wax onto a gourd. You may also wish to melt your wax in an old electric pan or heating dish with a low temperature setting. Paint brushes can then be utilized to apply melted wax onto your design.

Always be careful when using open flames, electric pans, and heated wax.

1. Candle, matches, wax, and kitska

2. Choose a cleaned gourd.

3. Cut or grate small pieces of beeswax. Place small amount of wax in kitska cup. Light a tea light candle.

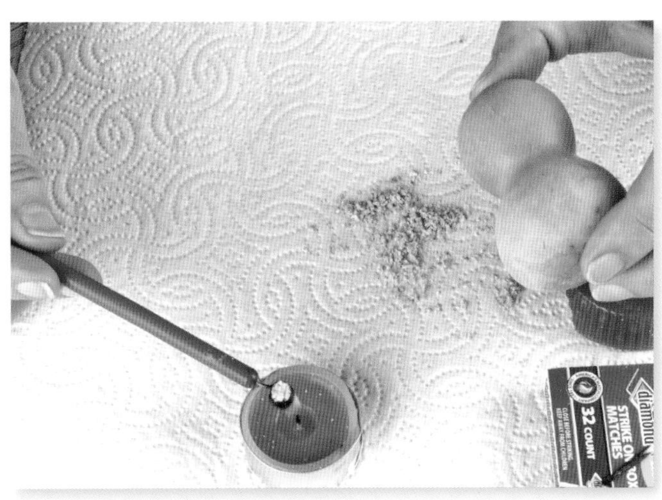

4. Move kitska back and forth over flame until wax begins to melt.

5. With kitska tip touching gourd, outline chosen design. Each time wax stops flowing, move kitska back and forth over flame and return to design.

6. Once wax design is finished, apply one or more coats of leather dye with dauber.

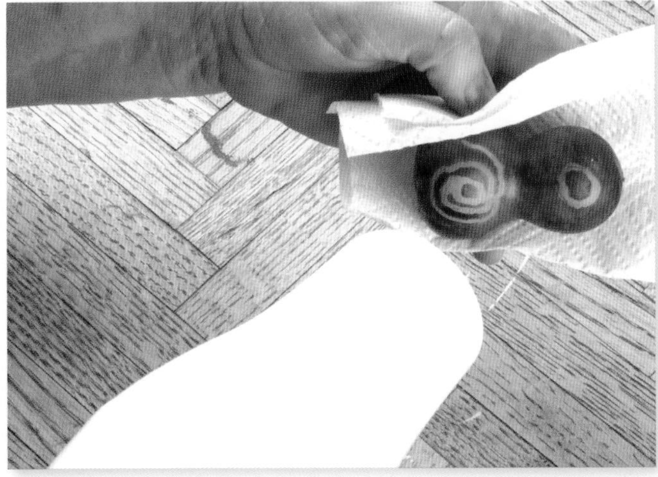

7. Hold gourd in layered paper towel and heat wax with hair dryer until all wax melts. Wipe off wax with paper towel.

8. Seal design with brush-on varnish.

GLUE

Materials needed:

- gourd
- hot glue gun
- glue sticks
- paper towels
- leather dye and dauber

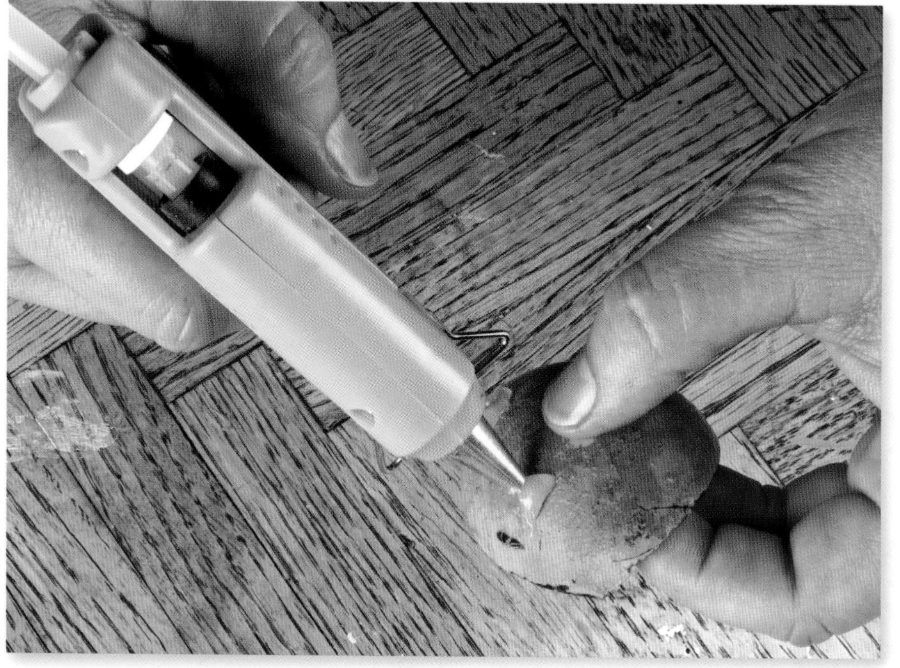

1. Apply hot glue with glue gun to create a resist.

2. Add leather dye and, when dry, pick off dried glue to reveal design formed by glue resist.

TWISTED LEATHER FRINGE

Materials needed:

- 5 to 8 inch or longer thin suede or smooth leather
- plastic cup
- water
- scissors
- wood board, larger than leather
- thumb tacks

1. Leather piece is cut into strips 1/8" apart.

2. Soak in water.

3. Twisted leather strands are tacked to wood board.

4. When leather has dried, cut holes from ends of strips. Dried leather can be used as needed for decoration on gourd.

PAINT

Paint offers a wide range of coverage. Any gourd can be painted. It does not need to be cleaned or cut. For full coverage, use a brush or sponge and apply two or more thin coats of paint rather then one thick coat. Allow drying time between coats.

2. Paint on outside of gourd can be applied with a brush, a sponge, cotton swabs, or your finger.

1. This warty gourd has been cut. Inside has been cleaned and is being painted with black paint.

Metallic paint gives an interesting look to a gourd surface. Most metallic paints need 3, 4, or more coats for a rich shine. For a different metallic finish, first cover your clean gourd with white acrylic paint and let it dry thoroughly. After that, only one or two coats of metallic paint should be necessary. Try this technique on a scrap piece of gourd to compare the finishes.

3. This gourd has three coats of black paint.

ALCOHOL INKS

Alcohol inks offer many opportunities for decorative finishes. Experiment on gourd scraps in addition to following the ideas shown here.

1. While touching surface of gourd, tilt alcohol ink bottle and allow ink to run.

2. Once first color has dried, allow second color to run down surface of gourd creating an interesting appearance.

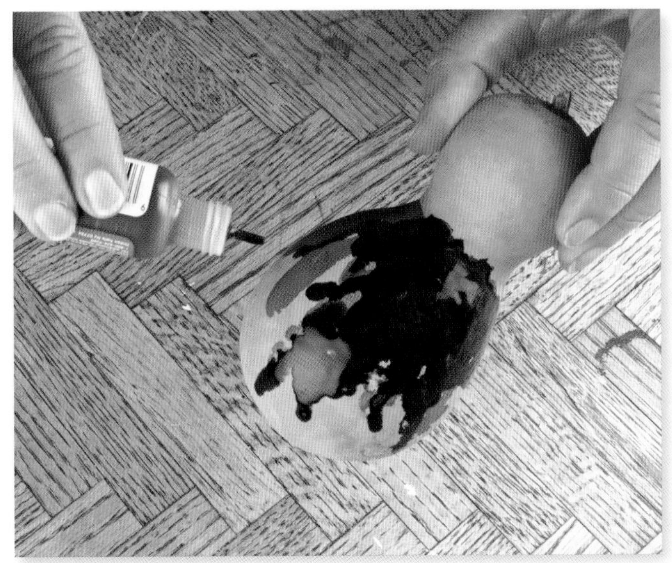

3.For a different effect, allow second color to run on top of first color while it is still wet.

4. Experiment with water or alcohol in a spray bottle spritzed onto an existing color for variations in shades.

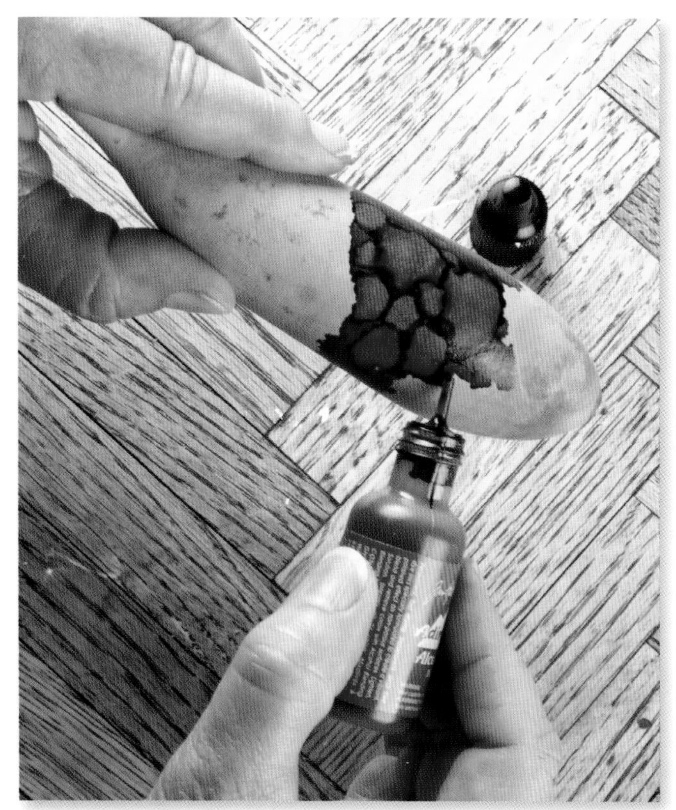

5. Drops of alcohol ink have been placed side by side onto gourd.

6. Here, drops of alcohol ink have been placed onto existing drops of alcohol ink forming dots within dots.

7. Finished gourd with numerous dots of alcohol ink.

8. Try adding the ink over a white painted surface.

RUB-ON AND SPRAY-ON COLOR

If you enjoy purchasing new products, rub-on and spray-on colors create unusual decorative effects. After searching the paint options, look in the scrap-booking, floral crafting, and model kit aisles for additional color components.

1. Rub-ons can be applied to gourd surface for a different effect.

2. Colored sprays can also create interesting designs.

SILK DYES

Silk dyes come in great colors and may be applied to a cleaned, light-colored gourd surface. Different results can be achieved by using a paint brush or wool dauber. Adding in assorted sizes of salt immediately while the silk dye is still wet achieves visual dimension.

1. On the left side of this gourd scrap, silk dye is applied with brush. On the right side, dye is pounced on with wool dauber. Continue daubing until desired coverage is achieved.

2. A small amount of silk dye is daubed onto white painted surface. Rock salt pieces are immediately put on each area to create various designs. When dry, brush off remaining salt with your finger.

LEATHER DYES

Gourd artists have been applying leather dyes to gourds for years. When using these dyes, keep these suggestions in mind. Leather dyes can fade, so keep the gourd away from strong light sources. It is also helpful to apply a clear sealer over leather dyes.

1. Multiple coats of leather dye were applied with a brush.

2. Leather dye was lightened with alcohol on second gourd piece.

GLAZES

Glazes can be fun to use, especially when applying with a gloved finger directly onto a cleaned gourd. Quite a different decorative result occurs when adding glazes over paints, dyes, and inks.

1. One coat of gel glaze was applied to this mini-gourd.

2. An interesting finish was achieved on this gourd when glaze was applied over alcohol ink.

Helpful Itemized Lists

More and more gourd artists are using materials from other arts and crafts to color and decorate their gourds. These embellishments can come from batik patterns and dyes, scrap-booking, knitting, weaving, crocheting, quilting, lace making, basket weaving, beading, paper crafting and leather-working. Other ideas may come from clay artists, sculptors, painters and photographers. You may think of even more applications than those listed here.

1. Acrylic paint, paint pens, and permanent markers.

ITEMS TO ENHANCE SURFACE COLOR

paint pens · acrylic paint · liquid or wax shoe polish · embossing powders · heat gun · oil pastels · transparent glass paint · mineral oil · glitter glue · alcohol inks · ink dyes · varnish · permanent markers · water color pencils · wood stains · paint pigments · spray paint · wood-burning tool and various tips · leather or silk dyes · spray lacquer · color waxes · gel glazes · acrylic sealers · rub-on and spray-on colors

2. Wood stain, colored pencils, and a sheet of colored leaf.

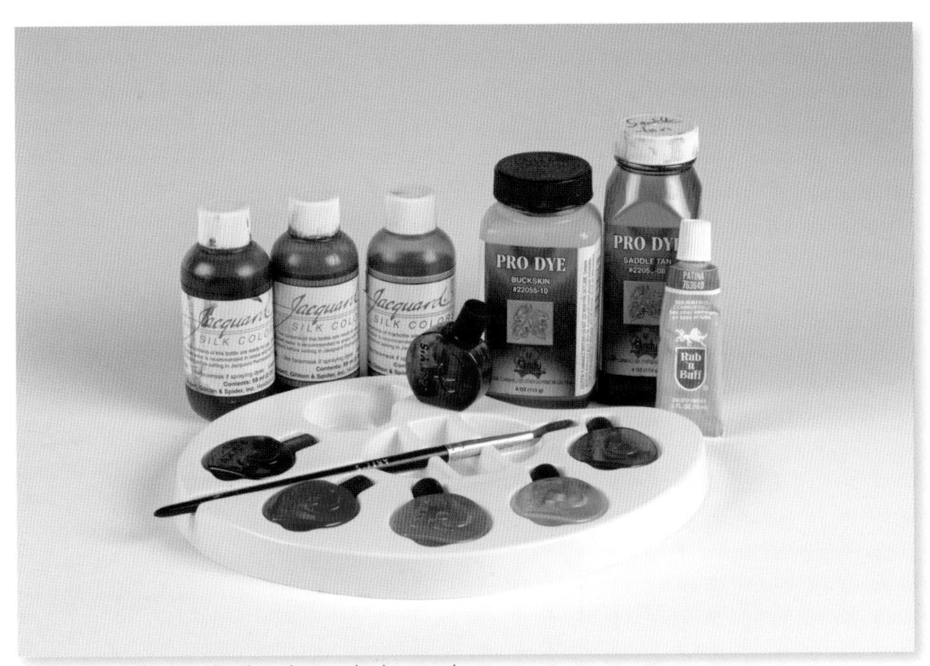

3. Silk dye, silk paint, leather dye, and rub-on color.

4. Pigment powders, shoe polish, and alcohol inks.

APPLICATORS

cotton swabs or balls · multiple sizes of paint brushes · foam brushes · wool daubers · make-up sponges or cut up pieces of a cleaning sponge · old toothbrush

1. Various paint brushes and palette knife

2. Toothbrush, wool dauber, sponge, cotton swabs, and make-up sponge

CORDING AND FIBER

braided cord · leather lacing · silk cording · waxed linen thread · yarn · jute · round or flat reed · sisal · raffia · ribbon · artificial sinew · hemp (any size or color) · sea grass

1. Different types of cords

2. Various lacing and paper cording

GLUES

epoxy glue · super glue · hot glue gun and sticks · foam glue · polymer glue · wood glue · industrial glue

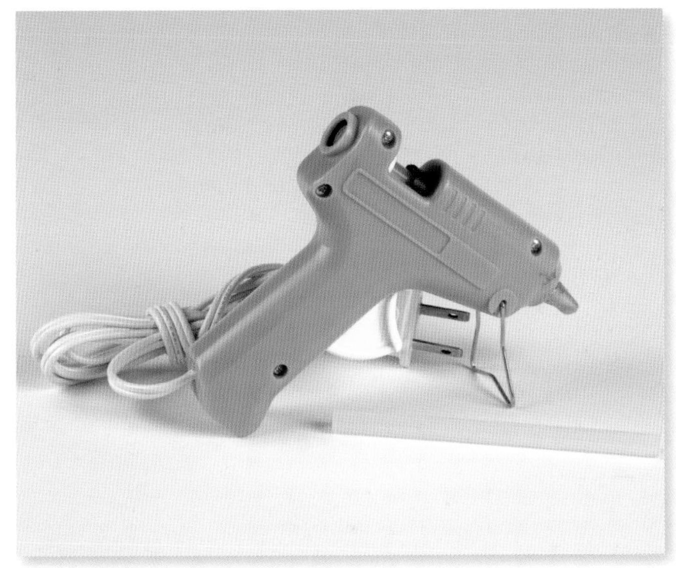

1. Hot glue gun with clear glue stick

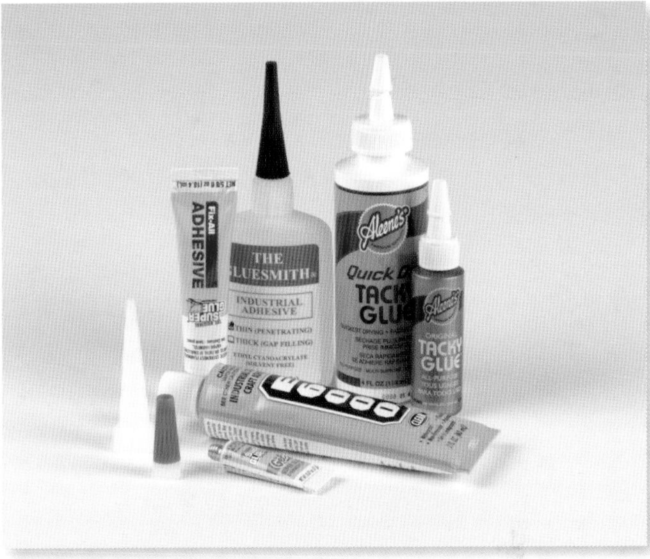

2. Assorted glues

PAPERS

wrapping paper · colored or white tissue paper · tracing paper · decorative napkins · decorative paper · handmade paper

1. Various decorative papers

CLAYS

polymer clay · kiln fired clay · air dried clay · flexible clay molds · glass cutting surface · pasta machine · clay oven

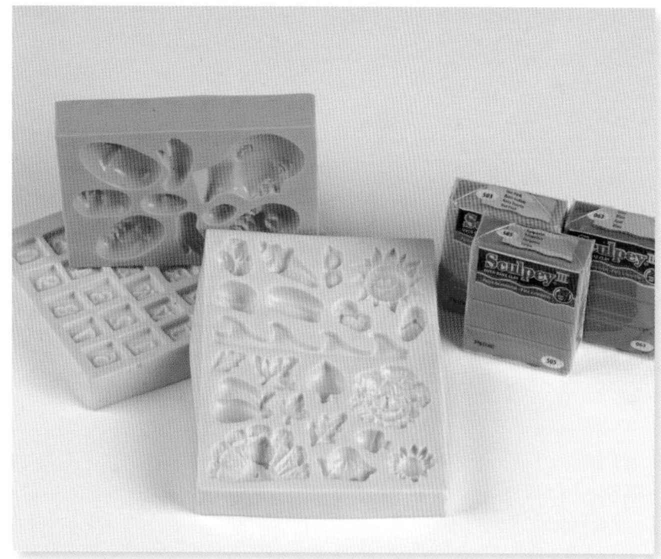

1. Molds and clay

2. Pasta machine for rolling and conditioning clay

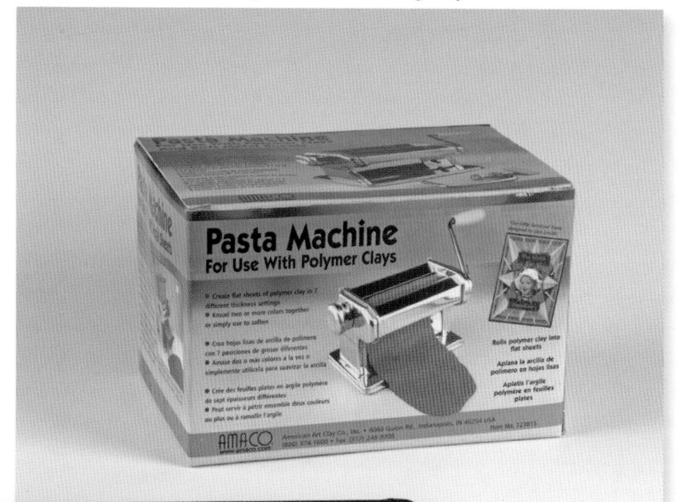

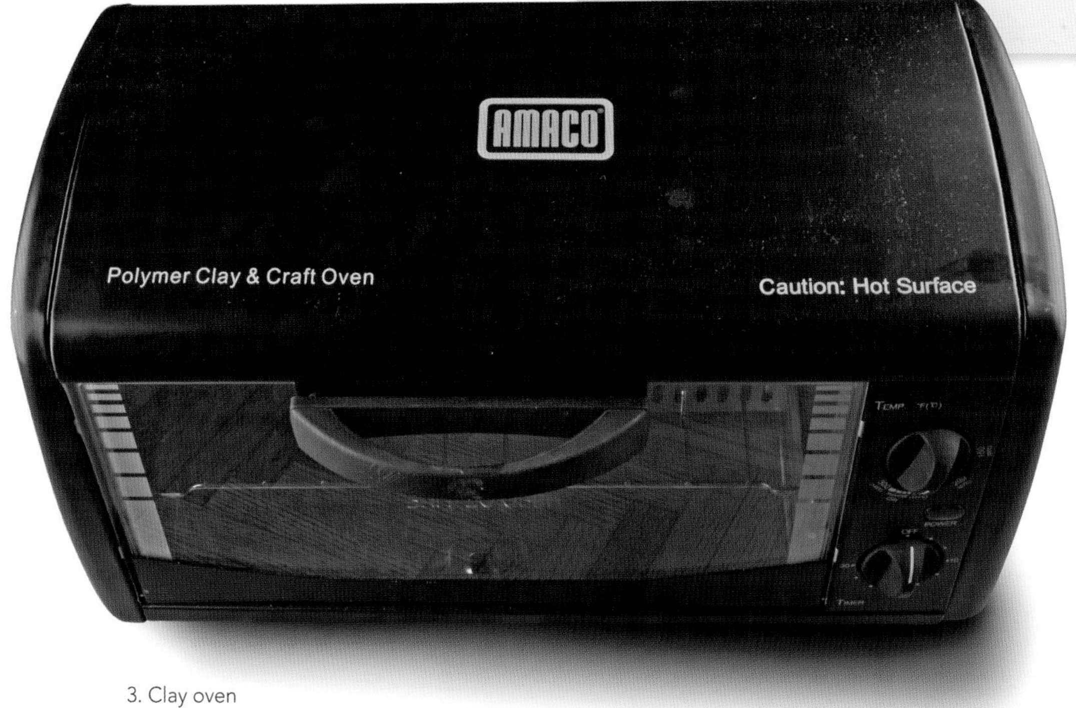

3. Clay oven

ADORNMENTS

carved gemstone pieces (gold, copper, silver leaf, or adhesive) · pine needles · costume jewelry · faux hair, eyes · foam cut-outs · scrap leather pieces · colored foil plus adhesive · dried natural items · pine cones · feathers · upholstery · thumb tacks · beads, buttons · silk flowers · glass or tile pieces · glitter · skewers · fabric · rubber or foam stamp images · grout · wood sticks · wire of various sizes

1. Colored wire, buttons, glass marble halves, and beads

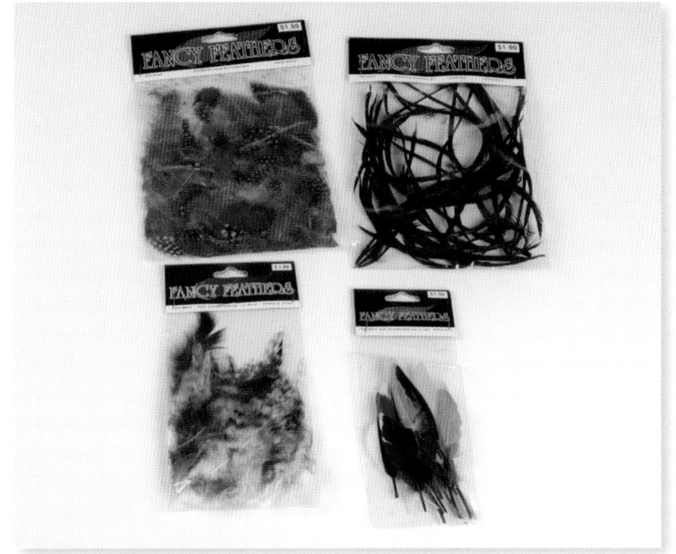

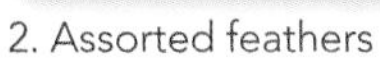

2. Assorted feathers

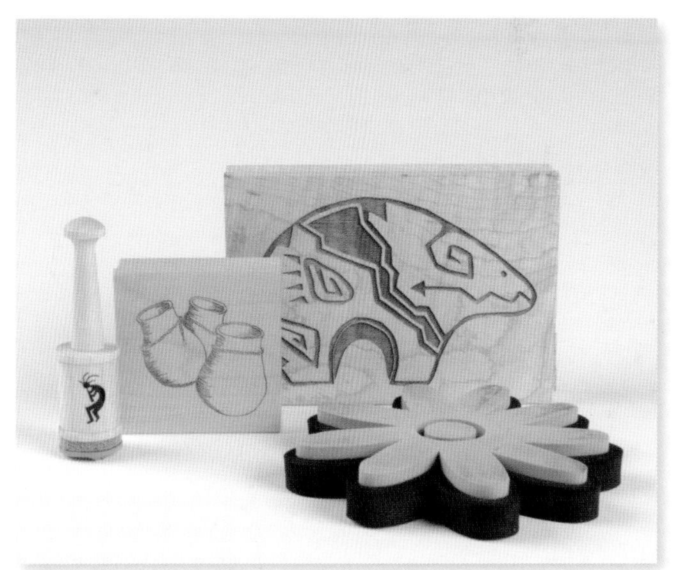

3. Foam and wood stamps

DRIED BOTANICALS AND NATURALS

bark · fibers · grasses · leaves · nuts · pods · reeds · sea grass · twigs · vines · wood pieces

1. Dyed sea grass

3. Colored reed

2. Dried pods, leaves, wood, and pine needles

4. Grasses, vines, and assorted fibers

Projects from Leftover Pieces (scraps)

CHAPTER 5

If needed, refer to Chapter 1 for help with cleaning, cutting, and puncturing.

When you begin cutting gourds, you also begin accumulating group scraps. It is a wise idea to keep those pieces for future use. The following projects are just a few of the ways to use those leftover gourd treasures. Enjoy these projects and also begin to envision your scraps in projects you will design.

First, though, one valuable use for gourd scrap pieces is making samples as you work on new techniques. Labeling and maintaining your scrap "file" will cut the time needed when you wish to use one of those techniques. You will already know how the technique works on a gourd and colored scraps can always be sanded or painted to cover old ideas or mistakes.

1. Stem pieces

2. Tops with stems

3. Broken gourd pieces

▶ TIPS for Scraps:

Consider using your scrap pieces of gourds or stems (all of which you have been saving!) to add dimensional design elements to a gourd project. You could stamp on a scrap, wood burn an animal, insect, flower, etc. and, when colored, add the completed scrap to finish your gourd. You could overlap various colored scraps and glue them to a rim to create a mosaic design. Your stem pieces could become arms, legs, noses, tails, or support for wings or other applications. A stem may also be glued onto a gourd that doesn't have a stem, but needs one.

4. Large and small scraps

5. Mostly cleaned pieces

6. Used pieces, still useful

Gourd Snow Woman

Materials needed:

- top of bottle gourd
- 3″ or larger wood base
- 1″ round wood ball
- white acrylic paint
- sponge
- 10 cotton balls
- (2) 1/2″ pompoms
- glue
- white textured yarn
- 2nd color textured yarn
- colored permanent marker

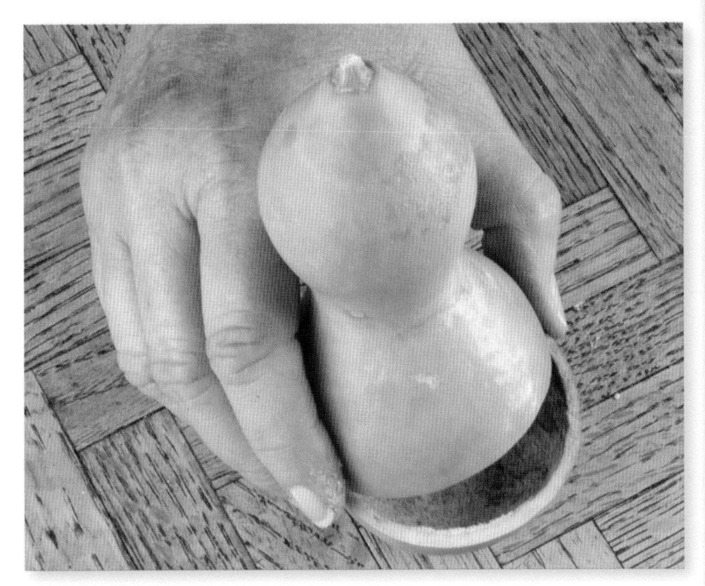

1. Cut bottle gourd, both pieces shown.

2. Gather cut top, bead, and wooden base.

▶ NOTE:

The next two projects were made from similar scrap pieces with wood additions. Many other variations may be achieved with this shape.

3. Glue gourd scrap top to wooden base. Glue head bead to top of gourd.

4. Paint entire piece white. Allow to dry.

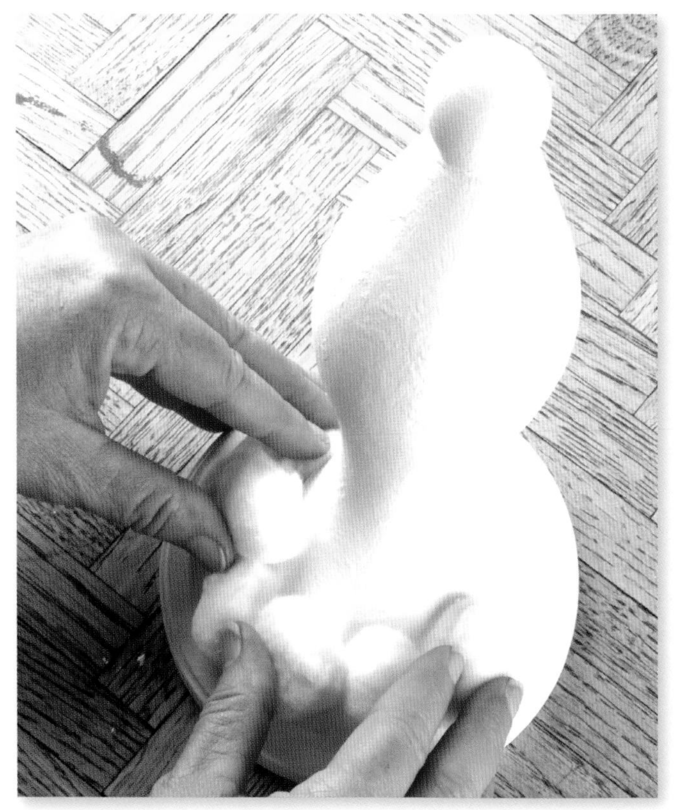

5. Pull cotton balls apart and glue to bottom of gourd where it attaches to wood base.

6. Cut yarn into three pieces, each six inches long. Tie around neck for scarf.

7. To make earmuffs, cut 2" piece of heavy textured yarn to use as connector between pompoms. Glue in place on top of head.

8. Glue one pompom at each end of yarn piece.

9. For hair, cut 12 pieces of white yarn that are each 9" long. Place 1/2" line of glue behind earmuff down back of head. Center each yarn piece on glue and press in place.

10. Using a marker, make 2 asterisks (*) for the eyes.

Gourd Feather Lady

Materials needed:

- top of bottle gourd
- 3″ or larger wood base
- glue
- 1″ round wood ball
- 2 colors of alcohol ink
- spray bottle of alcohol
- various feathers
- acrylic sealer

1. Glue top on base and glue head on gourd.

2. Dab lighter color alcohol ink around head and top of gourd. Spray or mist with alcohol to make color lighter and to spread color on gourd. Add darker shade alcohol ink to color rest of gourd and base. Allow to dry thoroughly.

3. Spray 2 thin coats of sealer over entire piece.

4. Glue feathers around bottom of gourd where it meets wood base.

5. Close up of base feathers and bead.

6. Glue hair feathers as seen on finished lady.

7. Glue feathers around neck for necklace.

Gourd Candy Dish

Materials needed:

- clean top of a bottle gourd
- small gourd scrap
- pencil
- hand or electric saw
- sand paper
- acrylic paint
- paint brushes
- glue

▶ NOTE:

If this project is used as a candle holder, a battery operated tea light is suggested. However, since we are using it as a candy dish, only individually wrapped pieces should be placed in it.

1. Begin with cleaned bottle gourd scrap left after cutting bowl from bottom of gourd. Cut off stem end leaving enough "neck" for holder base. Sand cut ends. Make certain gourd sits level.

2. Choose a smaller scrap. Cut circle approximately 1-1/2" to 1-3/4" in diameter. Sand edge.

3. Gourd scrap will cover opening in gourd base.

4. Place gourd circle over hole. Surround with at least 1/2" of glue. Allow 24 to 48 hours for glue to dry completely. If glue shrinkage occurs, fill with more glue.

5. Paint inside and rim with color of your choice. A second coat of paint may be needed.

6. Choose color of paint to decorate outside surface of gourd.

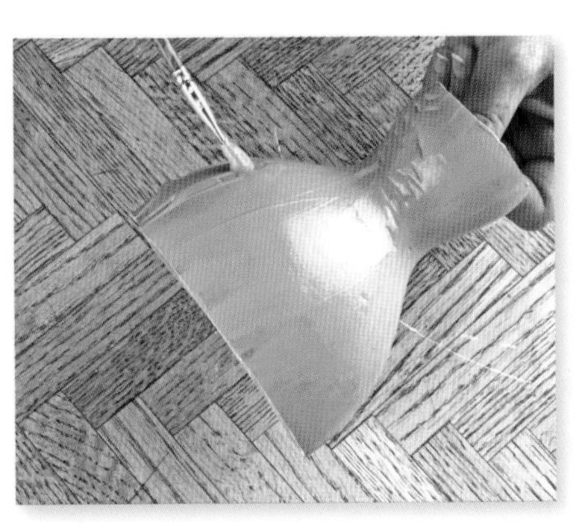

7. Multiple coats of paint may be needed. Decorative paint may be added.

Gourd Pin

Materials needed:

- 1 to 4 gourd pieces
- 1 pin back or tie tack
- 1 to 5 jump rings (12 mm)
- size 6 beads, 1 for each jump ring
- paints and brushes
- gourd seeds
- glue
- jewelry pliers
- awl or drill
- sandpaper

1. Choose three scraps that have already been painted or dyed. Sand edges of scraps and mark four holes with pencil. Drill holes.

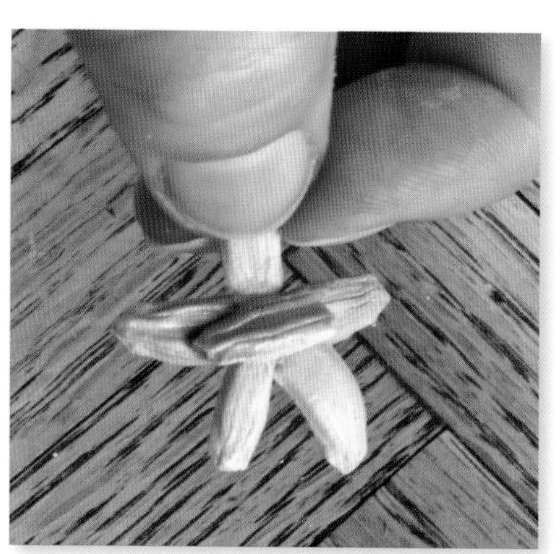

2. Glue together five gourd seeds in flower arrangement as shown.

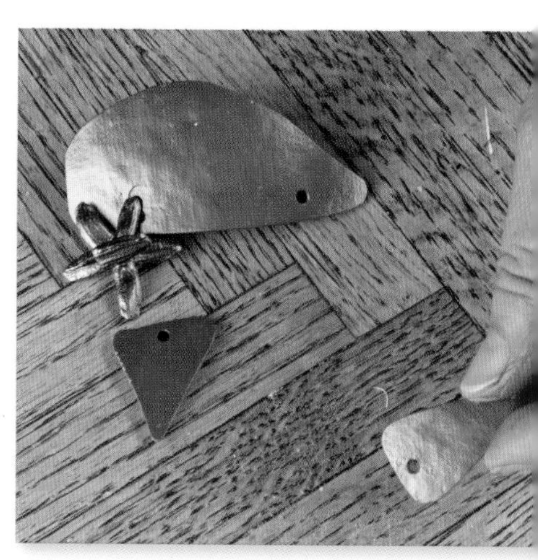

3. Using your choice of colors, paint fronts, backs, and sides of gourd pin base, gourd seeds, and dangles. Glue painted seeds on gourd.

▶ NOTE:

Jewelry projects are a favorite of many gourd artists because they are easy and fun to create.

4. Five stages for attaching jump rings.

5. Open jump ring back to front about 1/4" width. Place one end of jump ring through hole in gourd piece. Place other end of jump ring through hole in dangle. Place bead on one end of jump ring. Using pliers, close jump ring as evenly as possible. Glue ends of jump ring together. Slide bead over glued join.

6. Center and glue hinged pin back onto largest gourd piece. Be certain glue does not touch hinge of pin.

7. Tie tack pin style can also be used.

8. Alternate pin design with several coats of orange acrylic paint.

9. Finished gourd pin with white acrylic paint dots.

Big Brown Gourd Bracelet

Materials needed:

- large gourd scrap
- sandpaper
- alcohol ink
- jewelry pliers
- clear sealer
- awl or drill
- 25 jump rings (20 mm)
- (25) E beads
- 'S' hook for closure
- glue

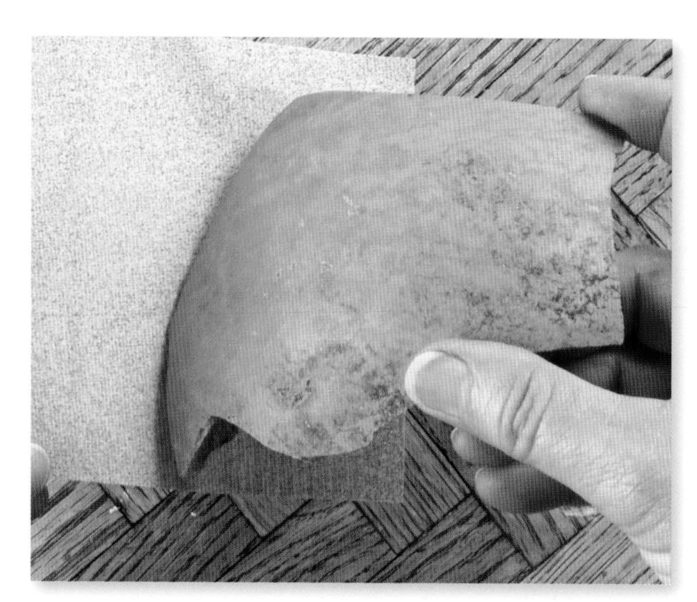

1. Choose gourd scrap large enough for your design. Sand sharp edges. Leave piece in natural or organic shape.

2. Choose an alcohol ink and then color edges and fibrous side of scrap (refer to Chapter 4 – "Alcohol Ink Technique" for bracelet side of gourd piece). Continue until all back side areas are covered.

▶ NOTE:

This bracelet will make a bold statement on the wrist.

3. Spray with clear sealer. Allowing a light mist to fall on gourd piece adds an interesting element.

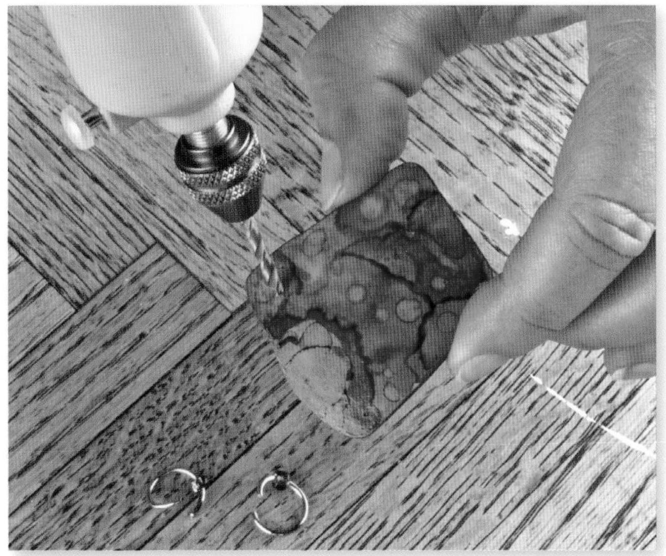

4. Mark and drill two holes about 3/4" apart at each end of gourd piece.

5. Attach two jump rings with beads in each hole in a link chain design. At each end of gourd, pull the last two jump rings together with a new jump ring and bead. Repeat at other end. Continue adding jump rings and beads to each end until bracelet links wrapped around wrist meet. Add three more jump rings with beads to one end for adjustable closure.

6. Attach clasp.

Gourd Link Bracelet & Variation

Materials needed

- 5 or more scrap pieces
- 12 mm jump rings (12-18)
- size 6 glass beads
- 'S' or 'J' hook clasp
- jewelry pliers
- paint, dye or alcohol ink
- brush
- awl
- craft glue
- acrylic sealer

1. Choose a large gourd scrap.

2. Break it into at least five pieces 1" to 1 1/2" long.

▶ NOTE:

A link bracelet made of gourd pieces can be whimsical or elegant depending upon how it is decorated.

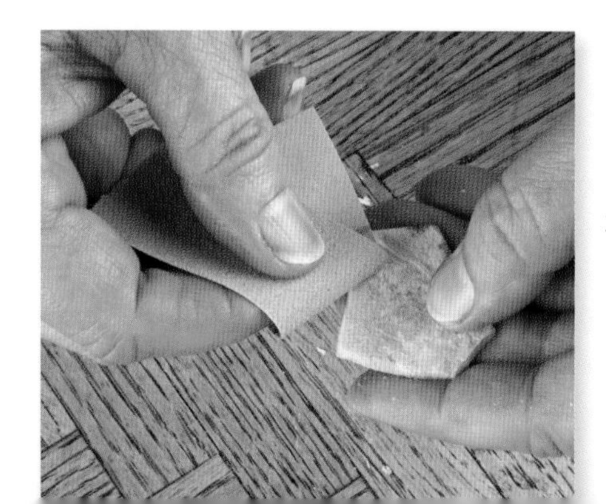

3. Sand all edges smooth.

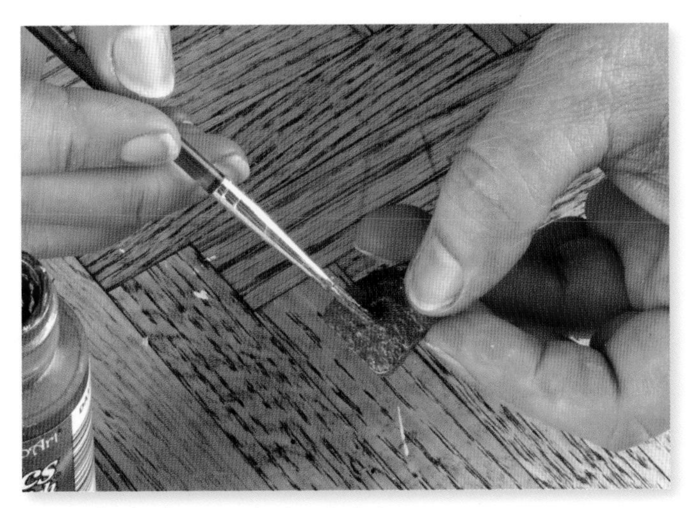

4. Paint backs, fronts, and sides of all pieces.

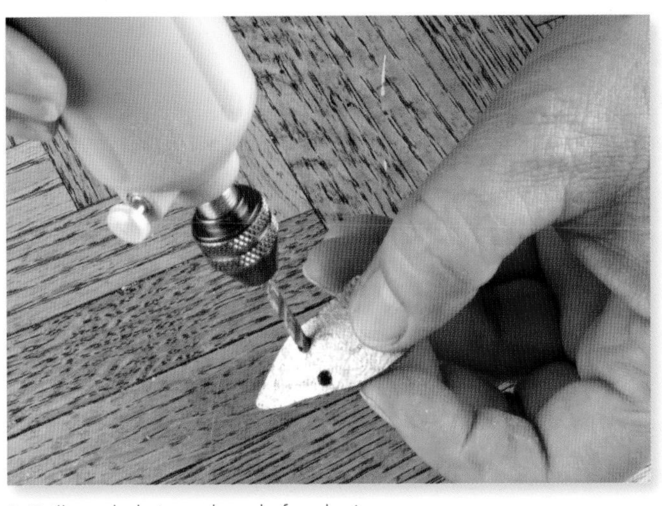

5. Drill one hole in each end of each piece.

6. Connect pieces with jump rings and beads glued over openings. Add link chain and clasp.

7. Alternate bracelet pieces – fronts.

8. Alternate bracelet pieces – backs with interesting texture

9. Connect with several links between pieces. Add chain links and clasp. Bracelet can be worn with either side showing.

Gourd Bangle Bracelet

Materials needed:

- 1/2" to 3/4" wide slice of snake gourd with a diameter of 2-1/2" to 3-1/2" to fit wrist
- sandpaper
- alcohol ink
- beads
- wire
- glue
- jewelry pliers
- scissors

▶ TIPS:

The 1/2" to 3/4" slice of snake gourd could also be used as a base on which to place another gourd project.

▶ NOTE:

All gourd pieces can be fragile. Keep this in mind when designing, creating, and wearing gourd jewelry. To help strengthen this bangle you may wish to coat the inside with a thin layer of air dried paper clay. Let dry and dye to match.

1. Sand a bracelet slice cut from snake gourd.

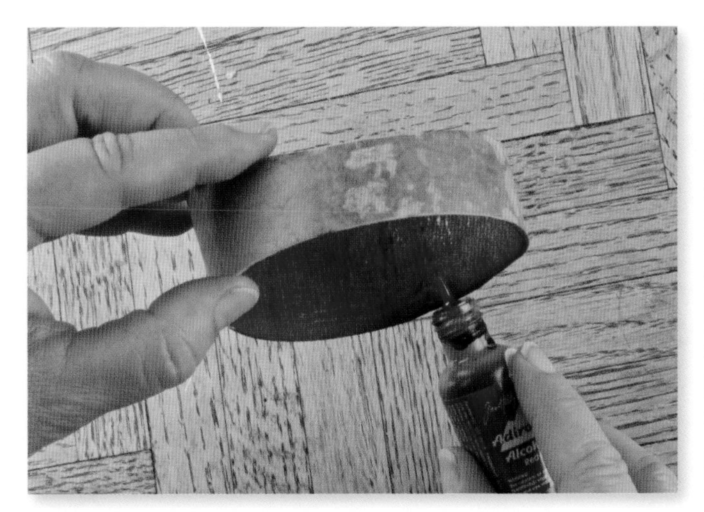

2. Color inside surface of bracelet with alcohol ink color of your choice.

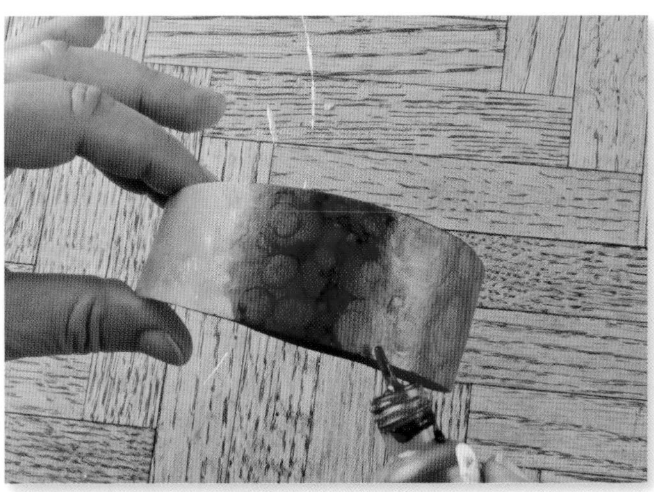

3. Decorate outside surface and edges with alcohol ink.

4. Bend one end of wire into nickel size circle and slide on 21 beads.

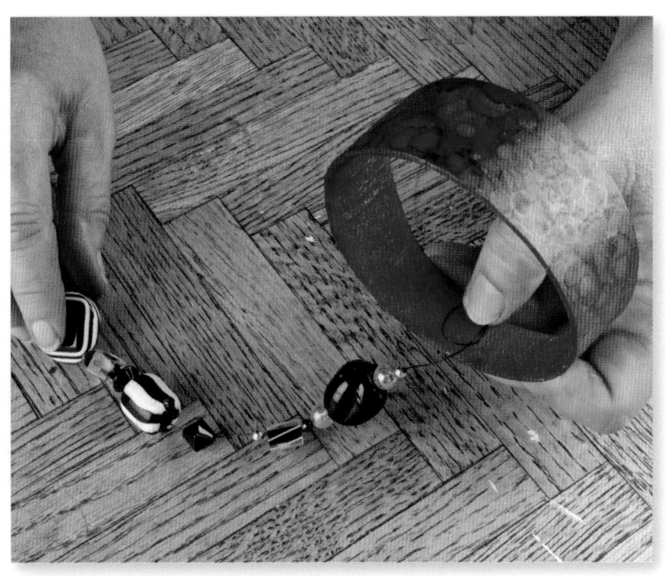

5. Designate where to begin and end wire inside bracelet. Hold circle of wire on inside of bracelet.

6. Slide beads 1" away from circle and move wire to outside surface.

7. Slide three beads along wire to rest on alcohol inked surface.

8. Pull wire tightly to inside of bracelet and move next set of three beads to outside of bracelet.

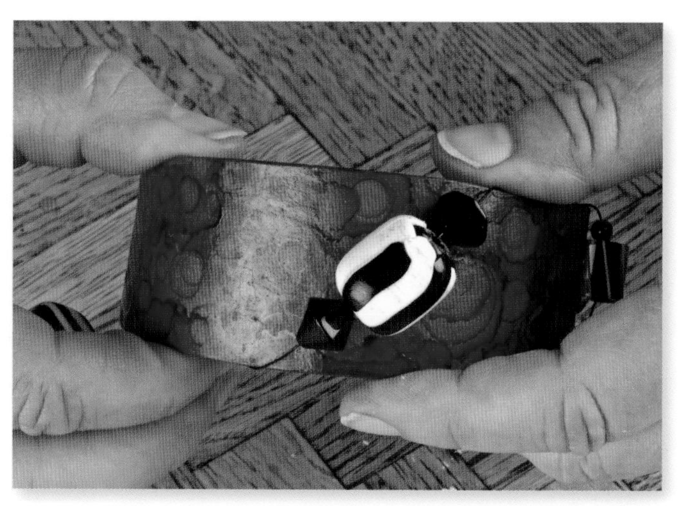

9. Depending on size of your bangle, repeat beaded wire design, 1" to 1-1/2" apart, five to seven times, ending where you placed circle of wire.

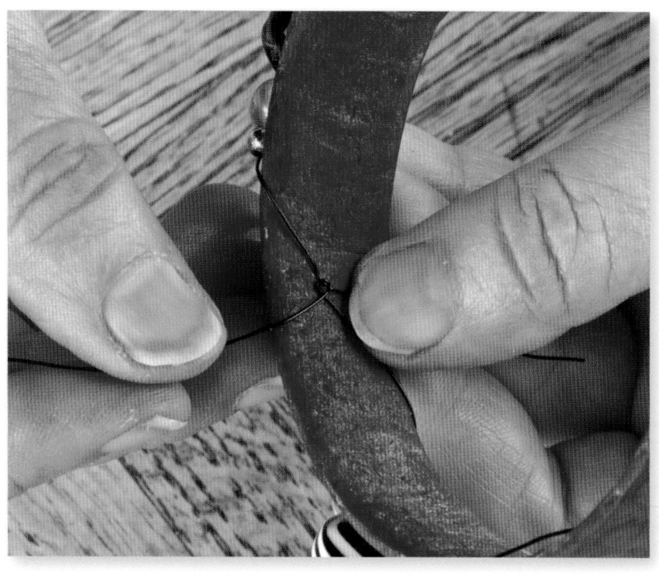

10. Remove any unused wire and cut ends to 2" or 3" each. Uncurl and twist two ends tightly together. Use needle nose pliers if necessary.

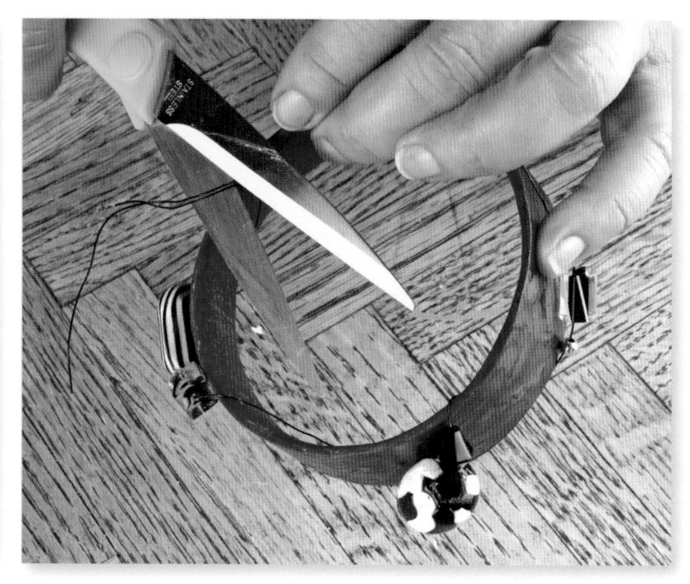

11. Clip twisted end to 1/2" and press flat against inside of bracelet.

12. Use glue to cover end of twist to protect arm from sharp wire ends.

Gourd Dangle Earrings

Materials needed:

- 4 small, clean gourd scraps
- sandpaper
- pencil
- awl or drill
- paint and brush
- jewelry pliers
- 6 jump rings (20 mm)
- (6) E beads
- 2 fish hook ear wires
- Glue

▶ NOTE:

Gourd earrings are especially lightweight, allowing gourd pieces to be combined in a variety of designs.

1. Choose four small gourd scraps and sand edges and backs.

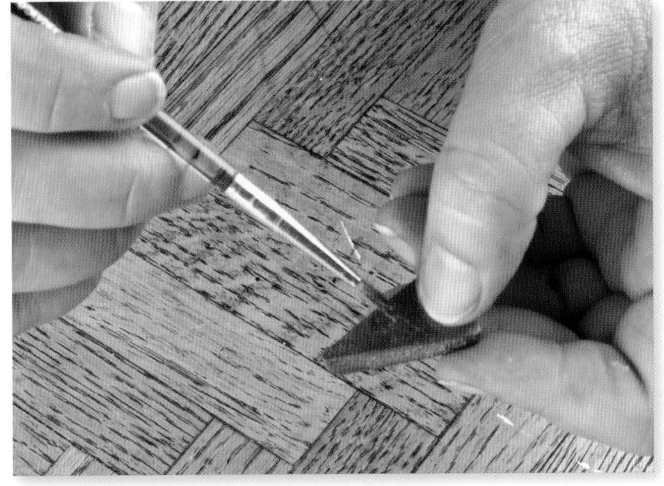

2. Paint all four pieces – fronts, backs, and sides.

3. Mark both ends of two pieces and one end of other two pieces with pencil marks for holes. Drill holes.

4. Add jump rings and beads to both holes for tops of earrings.

5. Connect bottom pieces to top pieces with jump rings and beads.

6. Add ear wires.

7. Alternate earring design with no dangles: Paint and then drill holes. Add jump ring with bead to each earring. Connect ear wires.

8. Finished alternate design earring.

Shadow Box with Gourd "Pottery" Shards

Materials needed:

- any size shadow box
- assorted gourd pieces and shapes
- assorted dry materials, stones, shells
- white acrylic paint
- additional acrylic paint colors
- sponge pieces
- glue
- feathers
- stamp

▶ NOTE:

This project can adorn any room in your home. Family treasures can be placed among the gourd pieces.

1. Open shadow box; put aside glass top. Choose one large gourd scrap and several smaller ones. Do not sand edges of pieces. Remove fibers from back of all pieces. Paint front and edges of all pieces with white paint. Two to three coats may be needed for complete coverage.

2. Choose a stamp with a design of your choice. With sponge, cover stamped design with black paint.

3. Place largest gourd scrap against painted stamp and press them together.

4. Design on scrap

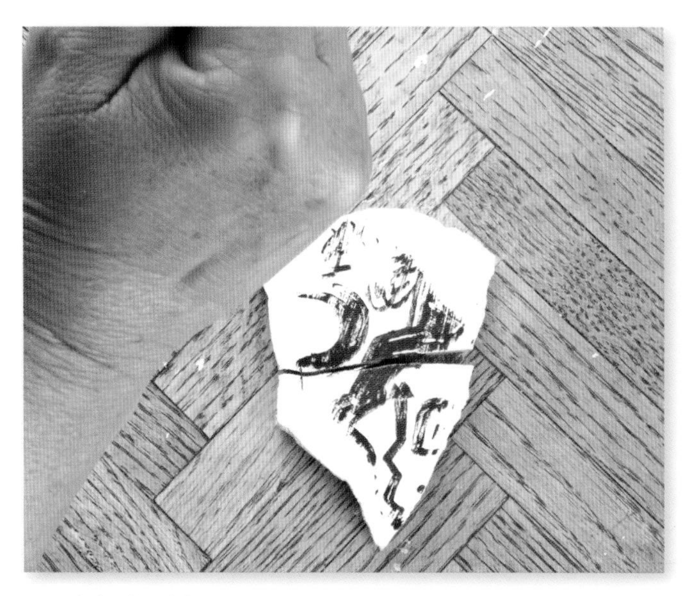

5. With fist, break large scrap into pieces.

6. Rub a thin coat of white paint over black painted design to give an aged look.

7. Arrange pieces in shadow box and then replace glass top.

Masks are popular around the world. The fun of mask-making is the unlimited possibilities for design. Any shape gourd, cut or whole, may be used to create a mask.

Though we reviewed cutting and puncturing techniques in Chapter 1, here is an alternate cutting technique for a Gourd Mask.

1. Draw pencil line from stem end to blossom end, both sides of gourd.

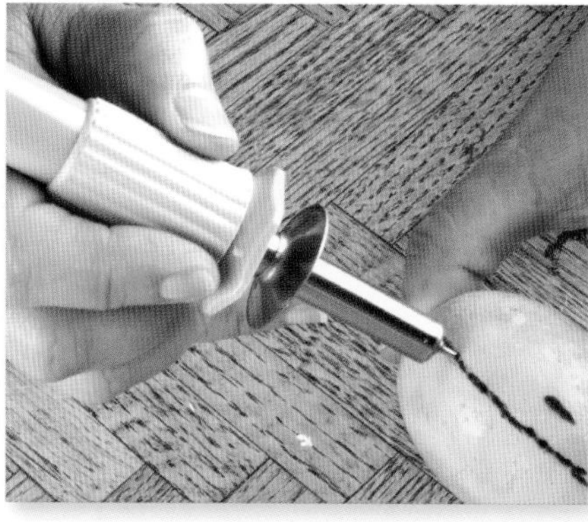

2. Woodburn a dark thick line over pencil line. Follow manufacturer's directions for use of wood burning tool.

3. Insert craft knife into wood burned line to start, and finish with hand saw.

4. These cut gourd pieces can be used for small masks.

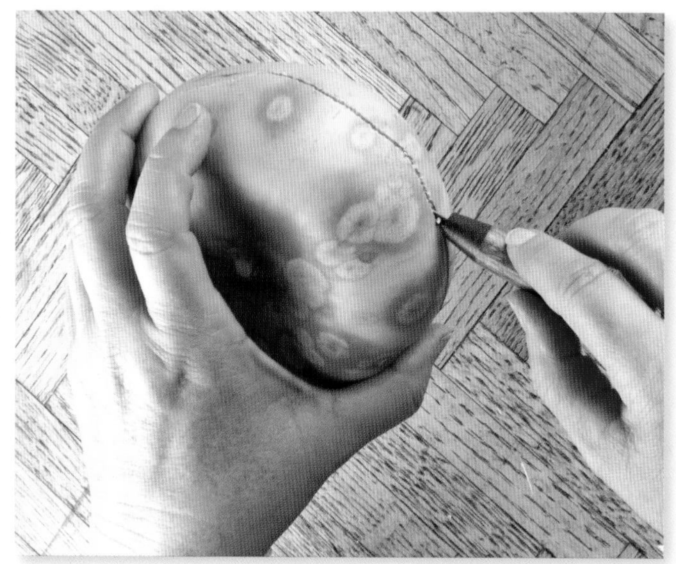

5. Canteen gourd with pencil line.

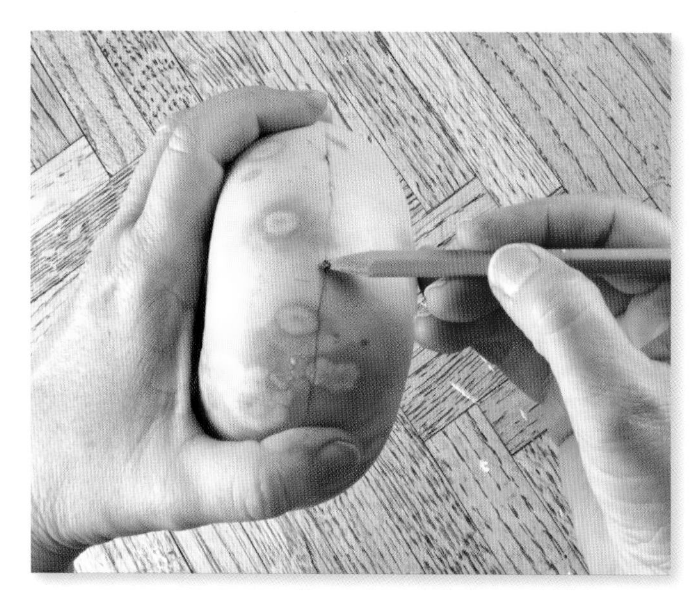

6. Canteen gourd cut approximately in half horizontally.

7. Two pieces of cut canteen gourd, top and bottom, can be used to make two masks.

Bead Face Gourd Mask

Materials needed:

- half of a cut and cleaned canteen gourd
- 40 beads, 8 mm or larger
- 26 gauge wire
- scissors
- sponge pieces
- (7) 1/8" dowels, each 12" long
- white paint
- wire cutters
- 1/4 yard coordinating cotton fabric
- glue
- drill, 1/8" drill bit

1. Clean outside of gourd. Cut and then clean out seeds and fiber. Paint inside with black paint.

2. Paint outside surface white.

3. Add as many coats of white paint as needed. Also paint first coat of white paint on all seven dowels.

4. Choose any of your favorite beads for eyes, nose, and mouth. Cut three pieces of wire eight inches long each and cut one piece of wire twelve inches long.

TIP:

Handmade fabric feathers offer endless possibilities for this beaded mask.

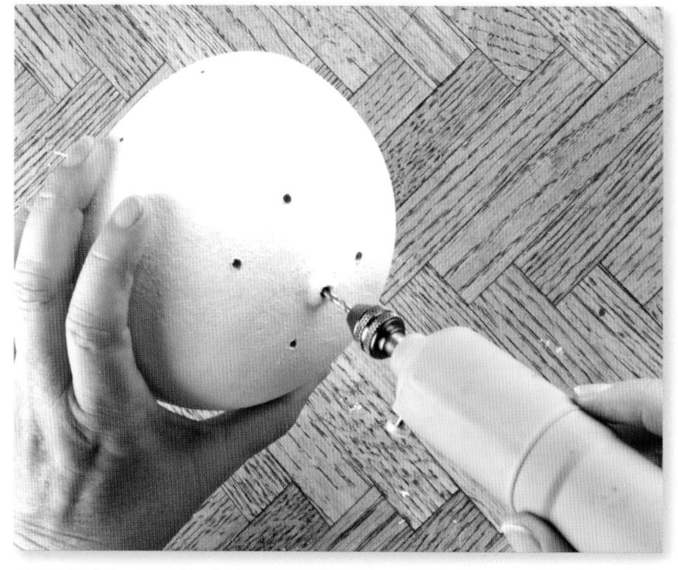

5. With drill, make five holes in mask, as shown for eyes, nose, and mouth.

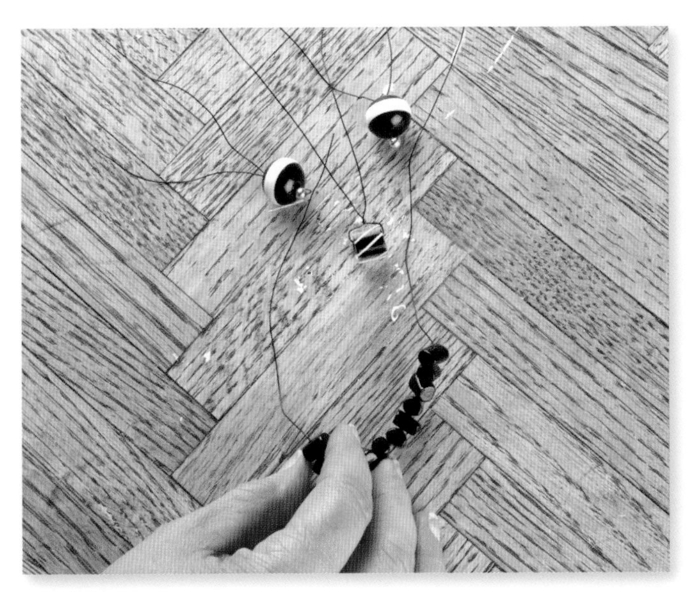

6. Insert three shorter pieces of wire in beads as shown. Use long wire for mouth beads.

7. Insert wire pieces into mask.

8. Turn mask over and secure wires by twisting together. Cut wires, leaving 1/2" and then press against inside of mask. Place a dot of glue on each wire connection. Set mask aside to dry.

9. Cut a thirty-six inch piece of wire. Slide remaining beads onto wire and make spirals around pencil, toothpick, and finger to space beads along wire. Set aside.

10. Return to mask and puncture seven holes 1/8" in diameter around top half of mask. Holes can be measured or placed randomly. At this point, purchased feathers may be inserted and glued into holes.

11. For fabric feathers, cut fabric into 14 pieces, 1" wide x 5" long. Cut ends of fabric pieces into V-shapes.

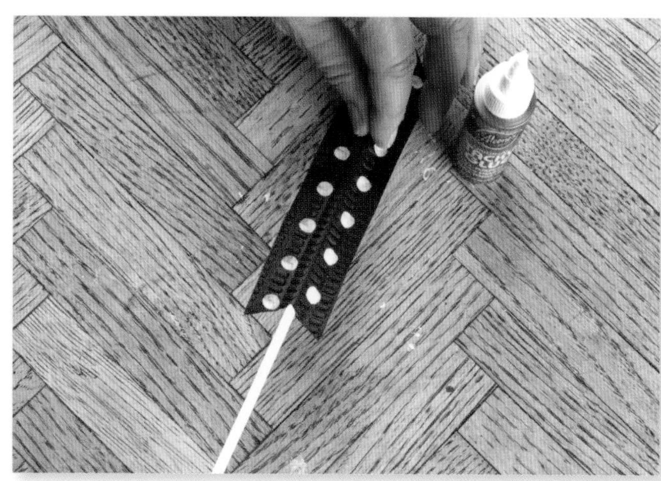

12. Begin with two pieces of fabric. Turn both pieces to wrong sides and apply glue. Place dowel on one piece and place second piece of fabric on top, wrong side down. Press fabric together. Repeat six more times.

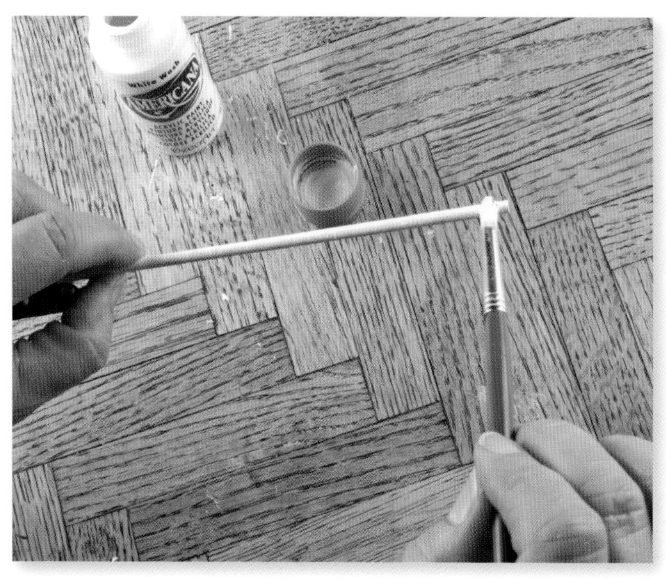

13. Paint second coat of white paint on ends of dowels sticking out of fabric "feathers."

14. Insert 24" piece of wire in bottom two holes of mask. Connect wire and secure. Wire will be used for hanging.

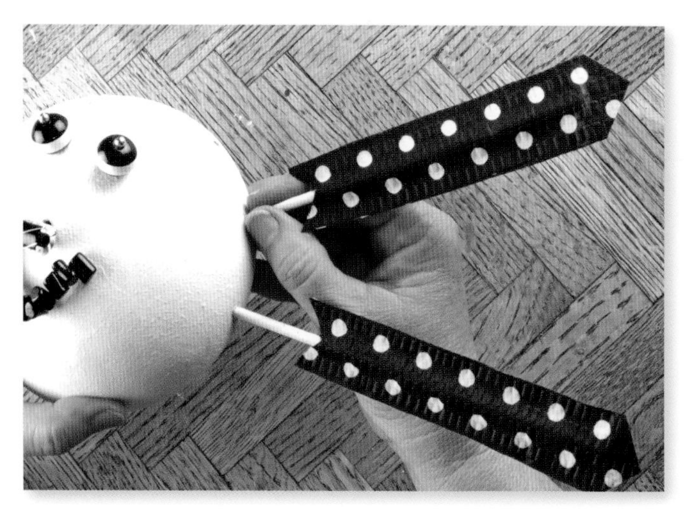

15. When feathers are dry, trim any rough edges with scissors. Place one feather in each hole around top of mask. Leave 1/2" of painted dowel showing. Turn mask over and glue dowels in place. Cut off excess dowel ends when dry.

16. Find middle of beaded wire and wrap loosely around middle feather. Wrap one end of bead wire loosely around two feathers on right side. Repeat on left side.

Sanded Paint Gourd Mask

Materials needed:

- cleaned bottle gourd
- measuring spoons
- 3 colors of acrylic paint
- small bowl
- fine craft sand
- craft stick and paint brushes
- 3" x 3" wood block
- scissors
- 3/4" wooden bead
- pencil
- 1/8" dowel, 12" long
- drill and 1/8" drill bit
- glue
- flush cutters
- 20 goose blot feathers

▶ TIP:

The dimensional effect of sanded paint creates an additional texture to this mask.

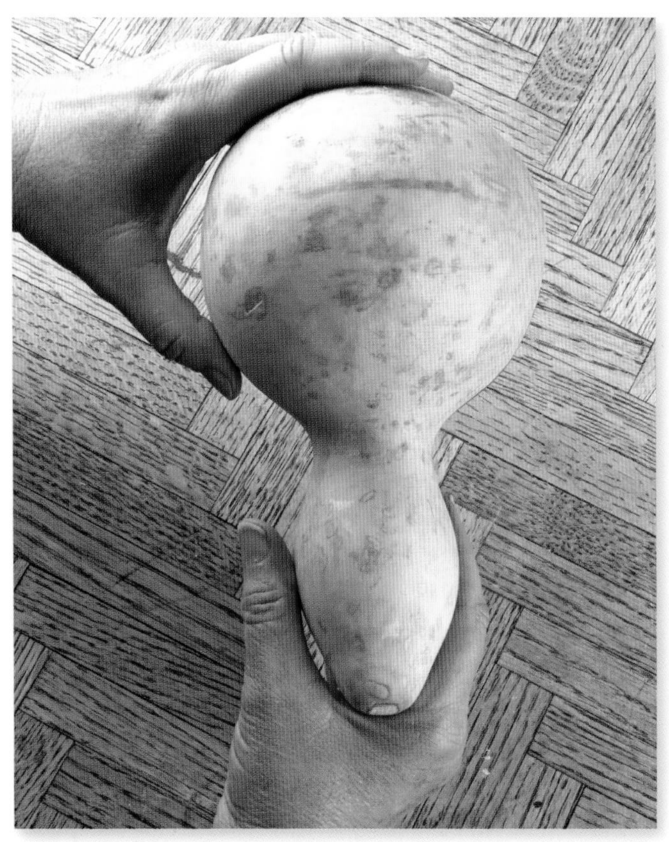

1. Choose a six inch to eight inch, cleaned bottle gourd.

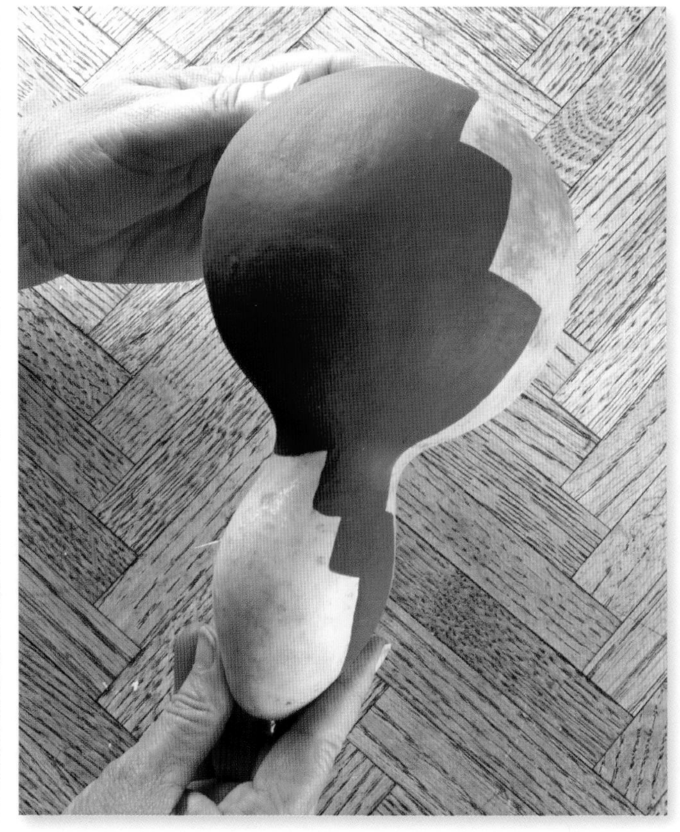

2. Sketch a design similar to one shown and paint design using acrylic paint.

3. Pour two tablespoons of acrylic paint into dish. Add one tablespoon of fine craft sand.

4. Mix sand and paint thoroughly.

5. Cover unpainted areas of gourd with sanded paint.

6. Glue together a four inch wood base, a wooden bead with 1/8" hole, and 12-inch-long dowel that is 1/8" diameter. Allow to dry. Cut dowel

7. Paint base, bead, and dowel with acrylic (unsanded) paint and allow drying time.

8. Using 1/8" drill bit, drill one hole in bottom of gourd.

9. Slide mask onto stand and glue in place.

Gourd Mask on a Tall Stand

Materials needed:

- egg gourd
- 4" x 4" wood base
- (1) 20 mm wooden bead
- hand or electric drill, 1/8" drill bit
- 1/8" x 12" dowel
- glue
- 2 colors of acrylic paint
- paint brush
- feathers
- contrasting color paint pen
- sponges
- paper towels

▶ TIP:

Depending upon the colors utilized, this mask can add a whimsical element to your decor.

1. Glue wooden bead to center top of wooden base and paint entire piece white.

2. Drill five holes in top of gourd and add a second coat of white paint to gourd.

3. Drill one hole in bottom of round gourd and insert dowel and glue together. Paint entire piece white.

4. When base and bead are dry, paint all surfaces with two coats of color chosen and set aside.

5. Paint gourd and dowel to match base. Allow to dry.

6. Using finished mask picture as guide, paint "face" on gourd with contrasting paint pen.

7. Glue feathers in cluster of holes in top of mask. Optional: add additional feathers at neck.

8. With contrast paint, using wooden end of paint brush, place dots about one inch apart along dowel.

9. Fill inside of bead on base with glue and insert dowel in bead. With paper towel, wipe off excess glue. Allow glue to dry.

Reversible Gourd Mask Necklace

Materials needed:

- mini bottle gourd
- 6" of 20 gauge wire
- puncturing tool
- 6 beads
- glue
- pencil
- paint pens
- markers
- paint brush
- drill and small drill bit
- necklace cording
- feathers

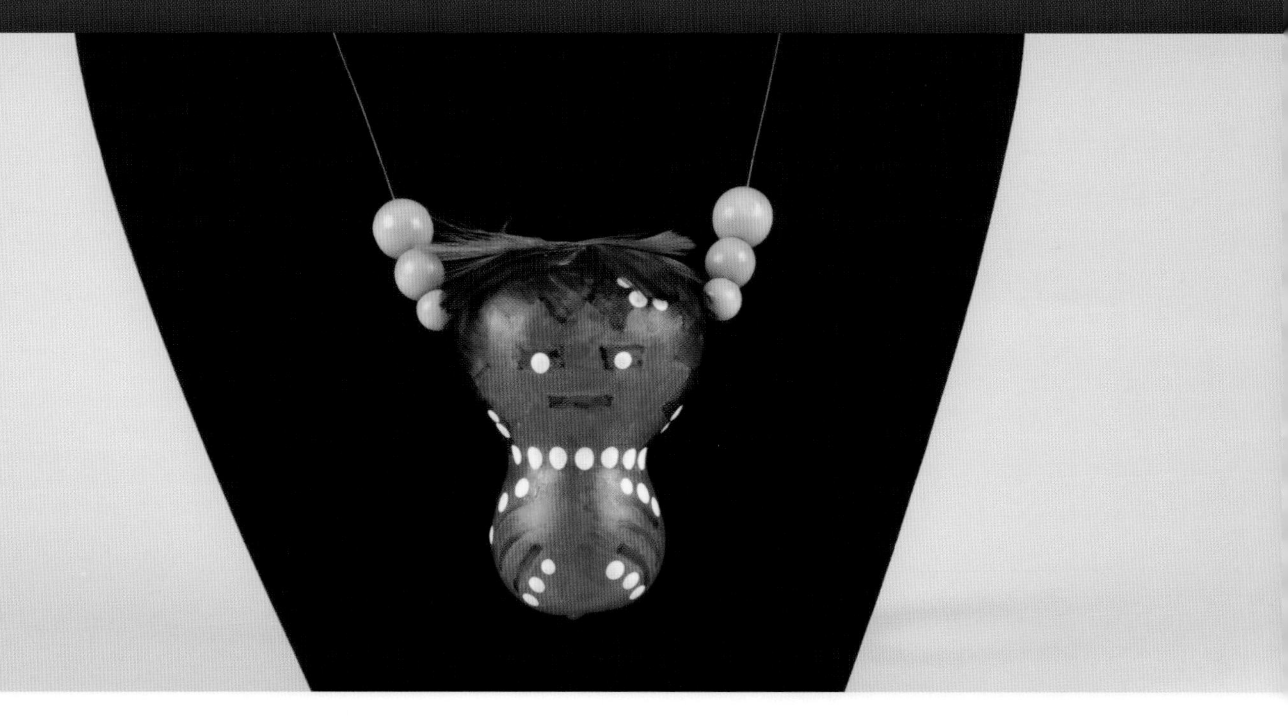

▶ TIP:

Whether you dress it up or dress it down, this two sided necklace appeals to all ages.

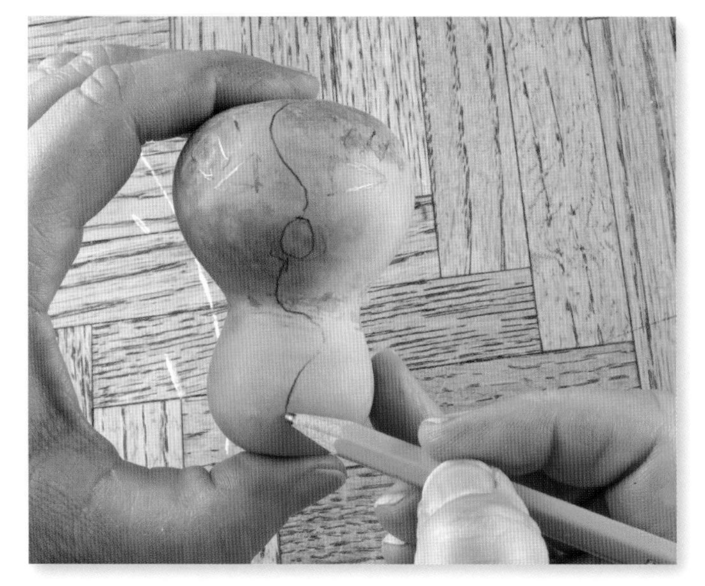

1. With pencil, draw a simple design on one side of gourd.

2. Draw a different design on other side.

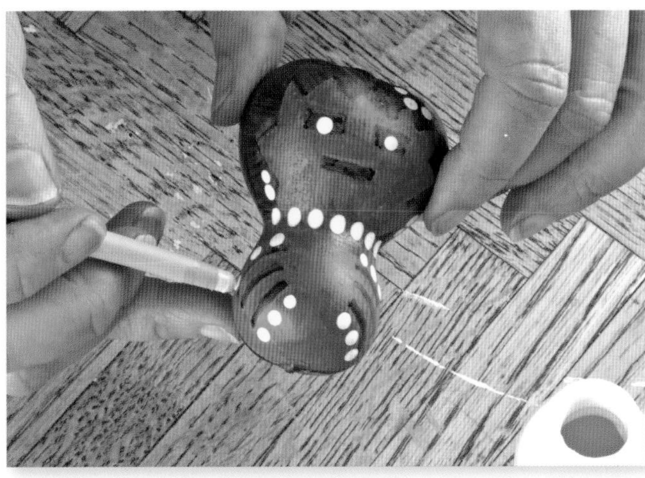

3. Using paint pens, color Side 1 of gourd. With white paint, add dot accents using wooden end of paint brush.

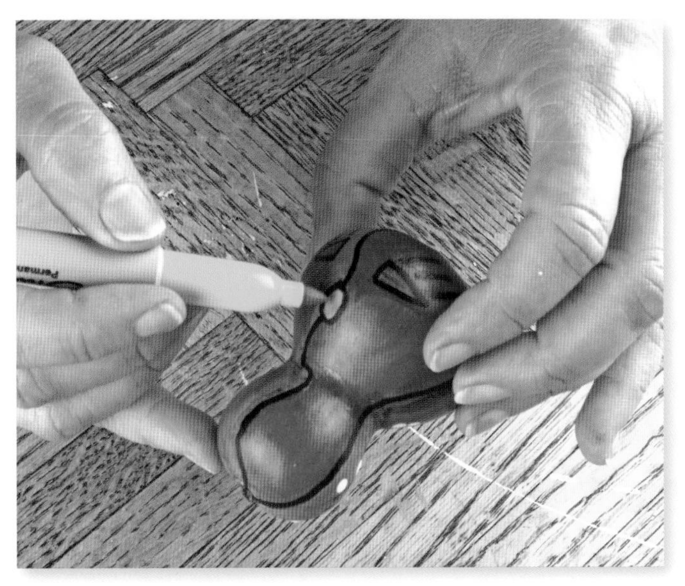

4. Paint design on Side 2.

5. Using 1/8" drill bit, drill one hole 1/3 way down on each side of designs.

6. Form a loop in the middle of 6" piece of lightweight wire. Thread necklace cord into loop. Insert wire into hole and pull wire and thread through both holes. Set aside twisted wire.

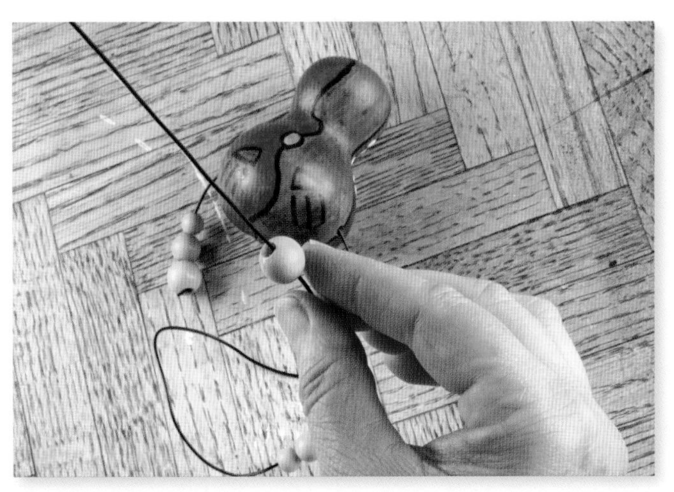

7. String three beads on each side of cord. Tie a knot at each end of cord.

8. With Side 1 facing you, place line of glue on head of gourd.

9. Add a feather.

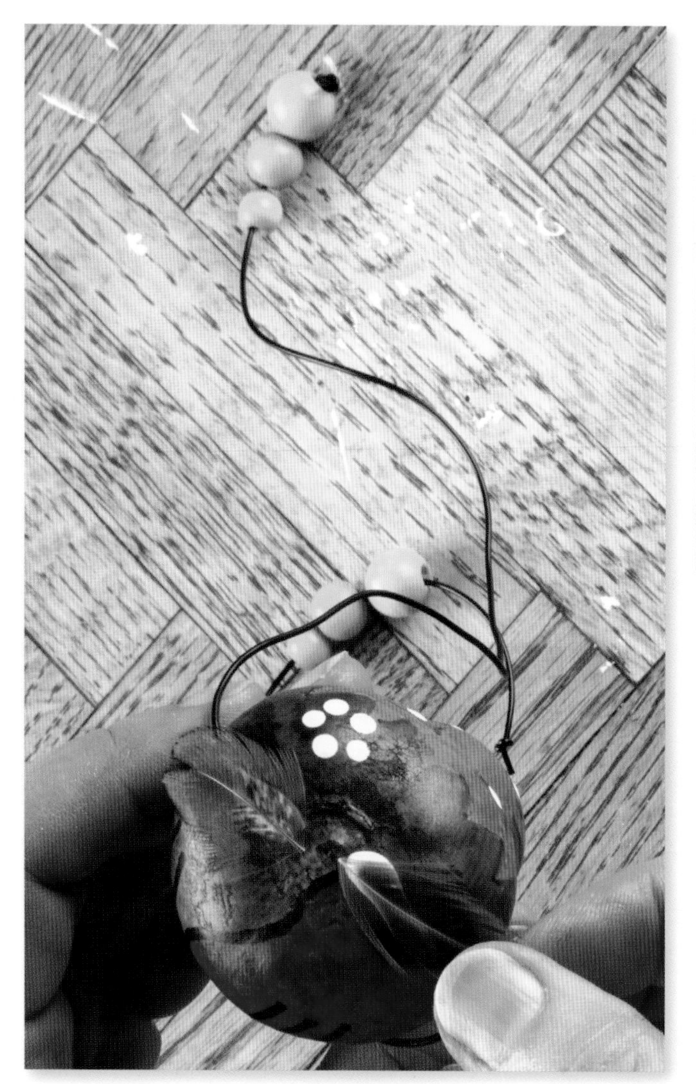

10. Add feathers to top of gourd, Side 2.

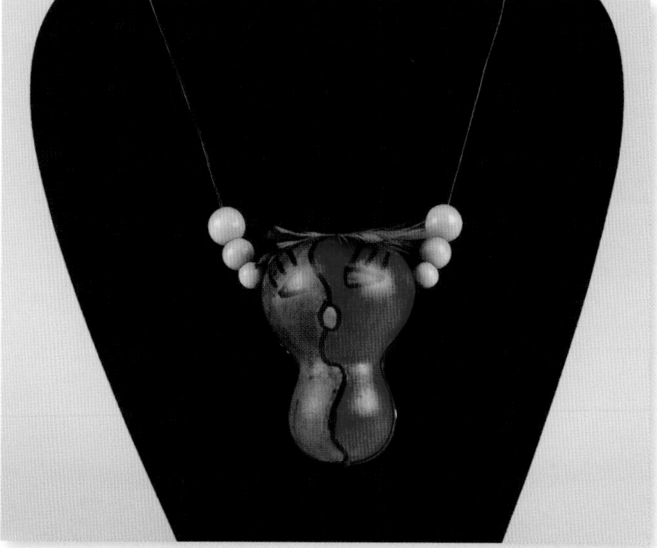

11. Necklace design, Side 2

Tricia's Gallery

"Guardian" – First in a series of tall, elongated gourd masks on stands, painted, and decorated with elaborate feathers

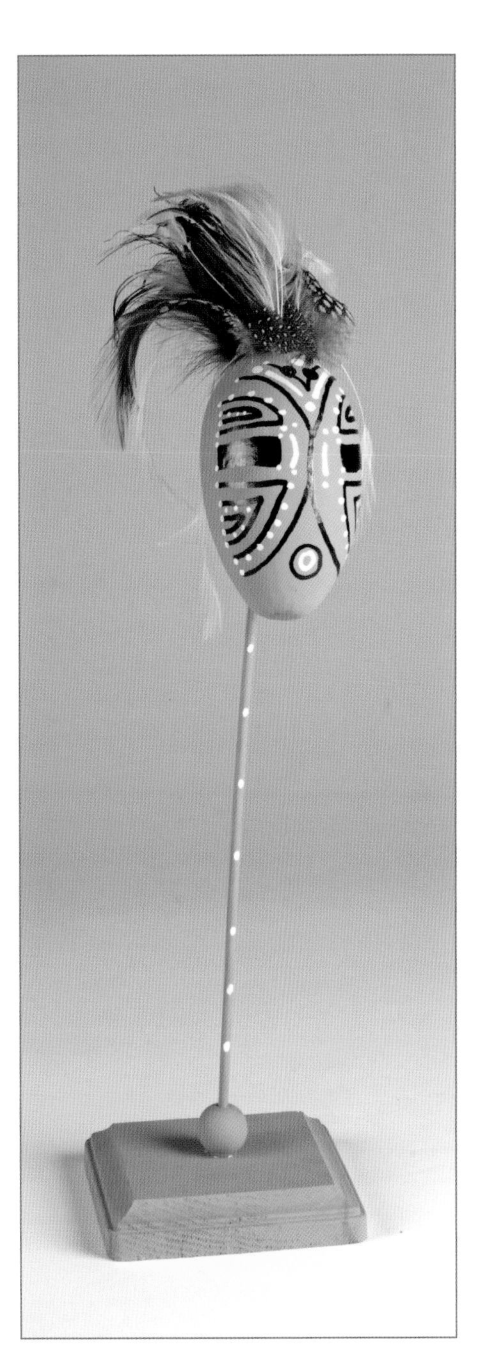

"Watcher" – Second in series

"Tall Blue Mask" – Painted round gourd on dowel and stand

"Shakere" – Dyed uncut pear shaped gourd with knotted cotton yarn and beads, finished with tied tail of yarn

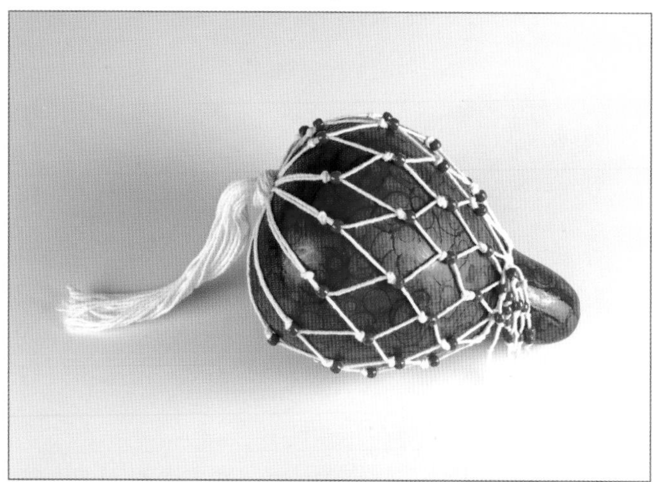

"A Mother's Love" – J-shaped snake gourd mounted on wooden base, multi-colored with alcohol inks, finished with feathers and small gourd bowl

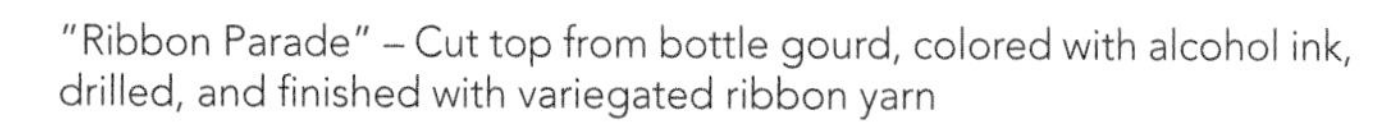

"Ribbon Parade" – Cut top from bottle gourd, colored with alcohol ink, drilled, and finished with variegated ribbon yarn

"Blue Salt Sea" – Pear shaped gourd, painted white, randomly colored with silk dye and removed rock salt pieces

"Storyteller II: Story Time" – Second in series, curved dipper gourd.

"Basket People V, VI" – Series of figures built on small, purchased baskets, adorned with colored feathers

"Copper Canyon" – First in series of masks with hand made fabric feathers accented with beads and wire

"Surprise !!" – Large, painted bottle gourd, decorated with natural botanicals, beads, and feather

"Ba-Bushka" – Painted bottle gourd, adorned with fabric and beads

"Petroglyph Man" – Leather dyed pear shaped gourd with wax resist designs

"Basket Woven Gourd I" – Matte painted, cut gourd adorned with feathers and woven with reed and sea grass

"Scrap Gourd Pendants I, II, III" – Series of scrap gourd pieces, colored with alcohol inks, drilled, and suspended on cords

"Pistachio Sundae" – Alcohol ink bicolored cut gourd woven with baby rush and specialty yarn

"Black Tie Optional" – Second in series

"Lady in Red" – Third in tissue paper series

"Blue Bonnet" – First in a series of tissue paper covered gourds, colored with alcohol inks

"Pride and Joy" – Large cut gourd, colored with alcohol inks, woven with basket weaving materials, finished with philodendron sheath

"Rushing Waters" – Second in tissue paper series

"Asian III" – Uncut gourd painted with several colors of alcohol inks

"Feathered Ornament" – Round gourd with attached feathers, bead, and leather strips

"Brown Desert" – Cut top of bottle gourd colored with alcohol inks

"Strawberry Jam" – Cut top of bottle gourd colored with wipe on shimmer paints

"Grape Marmalade" – Second in series

"Blue and Brown" – Long banana gourd colored with alcohol inks, drilled and woven with tapestry designs, finished with dried naturals

"Beaded Beauty" – Cut bottom of bottle gourd colored with dyes and finished with beads

"Raku Sunset" – Cut bottle gourd painted and finished with pigment powders

"Big Black Bracelet" – Scrap gourd colored, drilled, and finished with jump rings, beads, and clasp

"Green Fields" – Two scrap gourd pieces colored and divided by several jump rings and beads

"The Sun Kisses the Sea" – Five gourd scraps colored and separated by jump rings and beads

"Fish Ornament" – Banana gourd covered with textured clay painted and ready to hang

"Snowman Special Delivery" – Bottle gourd painted and adorned with baby sock, felt, and pompoms

"Snow Baby" – Tiny bottle gourd painted and finished with infant sock pieces and pompoms

"I've Been Framed" – Canteen gourd cut, painted, decorated with hand made fabric feathers, wire, and beads in 3-D frame

"Weaver" – Third in series

"Shell Diver" – First in a series of figures begun with cut bowl shaped gourd, basket woven, topped with alcohol ink colored gourd heads, finished with adornments

"Storyteller I: A Day in the Park" – First in series of long-handled dipper gourds colored with alcohol inks, adorned with different colored gourd babies, and finished with ribbon bow and feathers

"Black Bird" – Painted egg gourd with feathers and hat seated on small painted purchased vine wreath

"Gecko Climbing Sea Grass" – Apple gourd cut into bowl, colored with alcohol inks, drilled, basket woven, adorned with feathers and purchased gecko

"Golden Bough" – Various shaped painted gourds attached to purchased greenery